Bible Adventures

Bible Adventures

Gabe Durham

Boss Fight Books
Los Angeles, CA
bossfightbooks.com

ISBN 13: 978-1-940535-07-4
First Printing: 2015
Second Printing: 2017

Series Editor: Gabe Durham
Book Design by Ken Baumann
Page Design by Adam Robinson

For Cathy and for Ken

CONTENTS

Jesus entered the temple courts and drove out all who were buying and selling there. He overturned the tables of the money changers and the benches of those selling doves. "It is written," he said to them, "'My house will be called a house of prayer,' but you are making it 'a den of robbers.'

– Matthew 21:12-13

"All right, guys, this is gonna be so easy. All we have to do to make Christian songs is take regular old songs and add Jesus stuff to them."

– Eric Cartman, *South Park*

THE VOICE OF GOD

WHEN I WAS SEVEN, MY FAMILY moved from Springfield, MO, to Annandale, VA, so my mom could go to grad school and my dad could become the new preacher at the unfortunately named Falls Church Church of Christ. Since before I was born he'd been preaching in the Churches of Christ, a mid-size Protestant denomination known for its a cappella singing, full immersion baptism, weekly communion, and slavish emulation of the practices of the Early Church. Like the Baptists, a lot of Churches of Christ had in previous generations boldly claimed to be the One True Church and the Only Path to Heaven, but they were beginning to chill out on this point by the time my dad came on the scene.

I learned early on that we Christians and our wares were set apart. We had our own symbols—cross, fish, crown of thorns—and our own buzzwords, like "sanctification," "fellowship," and "atonement." You could throw these words around at church with a straight face, but you got the sense (or learned the hard way) they wouldn't play well at school. You were made to understand, too, that not everyone at school or in "the world" (as in: the *secular* world) went to church or prayed at dinner or would be joining you in Heaven, which was sad but necessary. Sometimes—you were warned—your peers in the world would Persecute You For Your Faith because of the influence of Satan, and that these doubters would try to trick you into not believing in God. But you had to keep believing in God because it was believing that kept you in Heaven, a clean place where your family was, and not Hell, which, not to like *scare you* or anything, was worse than the worst feeling you'd ever felt in your whole life, and you felt it for all of eternity, which is a billion years times a billion, only way longer. So believe, go to church, and buy Christian stuff.

Obviously you didn't have to buy nothing *but* Christian stuff. You didn't have to ask your grocer if the farmer who grew your onion was a Christian, but it was a pretty cool bonus if you happened to buy a Christian onion. And it wasn't like you couldn't enjoy the Beatles, except in the homes of a couple of sad kids whose parents were still mad over John Lennon's "more popular than Jesus" line. It was that you got bonus points for liking DC Talk, Michael W. Smith, or better yet in the Churches of Christ, instrument-free singing groups like Acappella.

The divide between Christian and secular provided leverage that was at times useful to a child of Christian parents. Asked by Mom to turn the music down? You could counter, "Mom, it's *Christian* music." Commanded by Mom to turn the video games off and do some homework? "Mom, it's a *Christian* game." And then, really reaching, "I'm learning about the *Bible*."

My church had a children's lending library that was basically just a little cart that got trotted out every Sunday morning, full of Christian picture books retelling some of the more parentally appealing Bible stories—more of them about the time Jesus duplicated sashimi for hungry followers than about the time Jesus resupplied the booze at a wedding reception.

To check out a book from the library cart, I think you simply wrote your name and the book's title in a little log and then brought the book back when finished. If this part of my memory is hazy, it's because I didn't often go in for books about the same stories I heard in church Sunday mornings and again in bonus church on Sunday evenings and Wednesday evenings. On my own time I mostly dug into my ever-expanding personal library: Choose Your Own Adventure, Roald Dahl, Calvin and Hobbes.

There were, however, two items on the lending library cart that were of enormous interest: NES games called *Joshua & the Battle of Jericho* and *Bible Adventures*. "FOR PLAY ON NINTENDO" read yellow text on a black bar at the bottom of each box—and then above it was the small pink logo for a company I'd never heard of: Wisdom Tree. I didn't care that these cartridges were black instead of gray, slimmer than a normal cartridge, or that they required you to cram the cartridge into the front of your Nintendo without pushing it down. I guessed it had something to do with the fact that these games were Christian.

I'd try any game once, and the fact that these games were free to borrow blew my addict mind. My local libraries didn't even lend out VHS tapes yet, let alone something as precious and expensive as a Nintendo game. Weekend game rentals ran you four or five dollars, a new game could be bought at 40 or 50 dollars, and yet somehow these had wound up on an honor system cart, being treated like something as worthless as a book.

So when I took the Bible games home with me that Sunday after lunch—hopes high, expectations low—I was pleased to find that both games were kinda fun.

Bible Adventures is a three-in-one platformer starring Noah, Moses's mom, and David. My favorite of the three was Noah, who must gather two of every animal for his ark before the flood. It was a game for collectors, a *Pokémon* before *Pokémon*. The gathering of creatures was an activity not so different than the slow, pleasing accumulation of Marvel Masterpieces superhero cards that several of my friends and I were racing each other to collect, carefully placing new cards in glossy sleeves in numerical order. In "Noah's Ark," I liked the job-well-done feeling of having both pigs crossed off my list the same way I liked checking off marks on the little list that said which cards I had and which ones I *needed*.

Joshua is an uglier game but it was one I could play for longer, a maze crawler where you're trying to collect all the little thingies to make a magic door appear. You shot music from your body, which first made enemies angry, then killed them. Truth was, it wasn't much of a battle for Jericho. It played out more like the story of a little man, buried in dirt, trying to sing his way out.

What I appreciated about *Bible Adventures* and *Joshua*, playing them for the first time that Sunday afternoon, was that neither was as mercilessly difficult as many of the games I'd lately been playing. For every well-balanced platformer like *Mario, Mega Man 2,* or *Bugs Bunny Crazy Castle*, there was a demonically challenging Game Over delivery device like *Ghosts 'n Goblins*. In those early days, games were pricey enough that I was allowed maybe three purchases a year and a rental a month. I'd pick up a game based only on its epic box art, die four times per minute, and be filled with regret for having chosen the Wrong Game. The few times I bought the Wrong Game or received it for Christmas, I was filled with the entitled child's sense of having been supremely cheated by the universe. "I could be playing a Konami code-busted game of *Contra* right now. Why did I take a chance on *Ikari Warriors*?"

The Wisdom Tree games were made of softer stuff, and I was okay with that. I wouldn't have paid Toys "R" Us prices for *Bible Adventures* (not that Toys "R" Us even stocked it) but I might've paid FuncoLand prices. Certainly these games outperformed so many lame licensed games like *Ghostbusters, T&C Surf Designs*, or *The Uncanny X-Men*. But instead I played the games for a couple weeks, dutifully returned them to the church cart, saved up for and bought a Sega Genesis, and for twenty years never looked back.

•

A year ago I started my own company, editing and publishing a series of books about video games. I contacted people I admired and asked them to write books for the series, and most of those writers said, "I know just the game I'm going write about." The subject of my own entry in the series was far less obvious to me. I thought about some of the games I loved best: *A Link to the Past*, *Chrono Trigger*, *Super Mario 64*. Perfect games made by Japanese guys I'd never meet in a language I'd never speak. But what did I have to say about *Mario 64*? It just felt good to play it.

And then I remembered *Bible Adventures*, a game I'd never owned that had been heavily marketed to members of a faith I'd mostly left behind. As I read every single article I could find about *Bible Adventures* and the semi-defunct company that made it, I discovered that, despite the fact that the game was neither one of my best-loved or most-hated, *Bible Adventures* had one of the weirdest development stories in all of video gaming's short history. It was a story that delved into plucky entrepreneurs, seat-of-the-pants coding, corporate muscle, horror movie rights, the Christian retail industry, and crises of faith.

But was there a book in it?

Hard to say when I got my answer. Maybe it was when game developer Dan Burke told me that nearly everyone who made these games was atheist or agnostic. Maybe it was when fellow developer Roger Deforest told me about the nights he programmed music for Christian games and then went out with his boss and coworkers to a strip club. Maybe it was when I read the old Warp Zone interview in which interviewer Dave Allwein politely tells Wisdom Tree founder Dan Lawton, "Well I really appreciate talking to you. I really like [your] games a lot," and Lawton replies, "You can't be serious."

A voice, from deep within or deep without: *You've found your book, Durham.* I'd been hoping my big idea would be for a classic game with a rabid fanbase that would sell a couple thousand copies on the title alone, not an unlicensed curiosity shit-talked by its own creator. But as Noah understood: When the booming voice in your head gets you stuck on a crazy idea, the idea's craziness is itself much of the appeal.

So when friends asked me if I was ever going to write one of these video game books myself, I started saying, "Yup! *Bible Adventures*."

And they went, "Huh."

QUALITY CONTROL

EVERY MAJOR EXTINCTION EVENT makes way for new life. The mass death of the Triassic period gave dinosaurs their big shot, the probable meteor that wiped out the dinosaurs gave us ours, and humanity's big population/resource splurge promises to wipe us out in favor of, well, something.

So it was with the 1982 collapse of the video game market: What struck Atari was not a meteor, but a spaceship occupied by a cute little alien named E.T. But every time he tried to collect a piece of his interplanetary telephone, Atari's blocky rendering of E.T. fell in a well. That was basically the whole game.

Atari displayed a toxic combination of poor quality control and simple human dumbass optimism. In May, they'd manufactured twelve million *Pac-Man* cartridges for the Atari 2600 despite that only ten million 2600s had been sold and that the new *Pac-Man* port looked and felt substantially worse than the arcade version. They were so confident in their flickery port that they assumed everyone who owned a 2600 would buy a copy and then two million more people would buy a 2600 system so they too could buy a disappointing *Pac-Man*. And now, with *E. T.*, Atari fell over themselves to get the game rights to the movie, guaranteeing Steven Spielberg $25 million in royalties, and then dumped the project in the hands of a small, well-paid programming team who were told they had six weeks. But as most National Novel Writing Month participants will tell you, not every creator thrives on deadline.

It wasn't only licensed games like *E. T.* and *Pac-Man* that sucked. There were also many awful Atari games made by third party developers: companies with no ties to Atari who independently created games for it. The sudden rise of third party developers like Activision had caught Atari off-guard because the entire concept of the third party developer had never existed before—Activision invented it. And after Atari's series of lawsuits against Activision failed, the courts confirmed that developers didn't need Atari's blessing to release games for the system.

In the case of Activision, this was good for gamers: Titles like *Pitfall!* became instant classics. But now that the dam was open, the sucky games flooded in: Mattel through its "M" Network division released nakedly synergistic bores like *Kool-Aid Man*, and Ultravision tried to get away with *Karate*, a one-on-one fighter in which the little loin-cloth fighters never actually make contact with one another. Meanwhile, Mystique brought us *Custer's Revenge*, a sociopathic nightmare of a game in which General George Custer dodges arrow attacks so he can rape a big-breasted Native American woman.

Another of those third party games from this era is what is believed to be the first Bible-based video game: an obscure platformer designed by Steve Stack for the Atari 2600 called *Red Sea Crossing*, about Moses dodging obstacles as he crosses the parted sea. It was packaged with both a coloring book and an "explanatory audio cassette" read by the developer himself. "Bible Video Game Brings Fun Home," promised the game's ad, though footage of the game tells a different story.

Our patience with Atari was at its end. How could a gamer tell which titles were fun when (1) Atari kept the bar so low for their own games, and (2) any developer who could code a half-passable glitchmonster could sell it for a quick buck? Gamers all over the world chucked their Ataris, Intellivisions, and ColecoVisions for good, and the unsold *E.T.*s famously collected in a New Mexico landfill, a fitting monument to the End of the Video Game.

•

From Atari's ashes rose Nintendo.

Nintendo's Famicom (or Family Computer) console was in every way an answer to Atari's failings: better graphics, simple and more intuitive controllers, family-friendly games, a peppermint red-and-white color scheme, and—perhaps most important—quality control.

All three of the Famicom's launch titles—*Donkey Kong, Donkey Kong Jr.*, and *Popeye*—were faithful ports of already popular arcade games, and Nintendo didn't hurry to fill the market with new ones. Over the next year, Nintendo slowly added safe first party titles like *Mahjong, Baseball, Tennis*, and *Mario Bros.* And when bad circuitry caused early Famicoms to break, Nintendo ordered an expensive recall of all Famicoms and replaced the motherboard in each. For Nintendo, doing it right was more important than doing it quickly.

Unlike Atari, Nintendo welcomed third party developers, but only when they played by Nintendo's rules. So developers simply went their own way, creating unlicensed games that could be played on the Famicom without Nintendo's blessing. And there was nothing Nintendo could do about it.

When they made plans to design a Famicom for the West, Nintendo made several changes to what would become the Nintendo Entertainment System (NES): They made the controllers unpluggable, rounded the controller's square buttons, overhauled the bright design in favor of a serious gray VCR look, and bundled many systems with a stupid, barely-functioning robot.

The least perceptible change, and the one most important to our story, is what's known as the 10NES lockout system: Before booting up a game, a microchip in the NES would check for a particular microchip in the game cartridge. If it was a match, the microchips would kiss and their love would spark the game to life. If it wasn't a match: LOCKOUT. Only Nintendo knew the 10NES chip's secret recipe, and they weren't sharing it with anyone.

The chip allowed Nintendo's president, Hiroshi Yamauchi, to maintain his company's family-friendly image abroad, and allowed Nintendo to market directly to the NES's target demographic—children—through the use of heavy censorship. According to content guidelines, Nintendo of America did not approve of games with nudity, rape, "sexually suggestive or explicit content," sexism, gratuitous violence, "graphic illustration of death," excessive force in sports games, "ethnic, religious, nationalistic, or sexual stereotypes of language," profanity, drugs, booze, smoking, or politics.

It was these standards that would change *Punch-Out!!*'s Vodka Drunkenski to Soda Popinski, rename *Wolfenstein 3-D*'s Hitler to "Staatsmeister," clothe the boobs on *Castlevania IV*'s nude statues, recolor *Mortal Kombat*'s blood to sweat, and alter the line of *Maniac Mansion*'s Nurse Edna from "I should have tied you to my bed, cutie," to, "Just wait until I talk to your mother."

Not to mention the reverse-miracle of transforming every bar and beer into a café and coffee in countless games such as *Chrono Trigger, EarthBound,* and *Final Fantasy VI*. Taken together, Japanese games ported to America resonate with a weirdly pleasing, almost Lynchian fetishization of coffee and soda.

"People from Nintendo […] insist that their standards are not intended to make their products bland, but that is the inevitable result," wrote Douglas Crockford in a 1993 *Wired* article, not long after his company oversaw *Maniac Mansion*'s conversion from Commodore 64 to NES. He concluded, "Nintendo is a jealous god."

But Nintendo wasn't just a New Testament God bent on filling his games with peace and temperance. It was also an Old Testament God of might and—when necessary—wrath.

Typically, the process went like this: LucasArts approaches Nintendo with *Maniac Mansion*, taking care to remember that they as a third party developer are only allowed to release five games with Nintendo per year. Nintendo accepts the game but requests (demands) content changes, and brokenhearted developers like Crockford comply. Once Nintendo is happy, they set the release date, choose the number of cartridges to be manufactured, and then manufacture the cartridges themselves, selling the cartridges back to LucasArts at a high price. Nintendo then controls how and how much the game will be hyped in *Nintendo Power* magazine. Last, the game remains exclusive to the NES for at least two years. For the third party developer's reverence, Nintendo anoints every copy of the game with the Original Nintendo Seal of Quality and, it goes without saying, a 10NES chip that allows the game to work at all.

Nintendo held all the cards. It was good to be God.

Until they didn't and it wasn't.

•

An NES console is just a piece of hardware. Nintendo built it to look like a somber VCR instead of a candy-colored toy because it pretty much *was* a VCR—the games themselves were the fun part—and even those, with few exceptions came only in Pallid Tank Gray. Just as anyone could legally manufacture a videotape, anyone could legally manufacture a Nintendo game. As long as they could get around the pesky 10NES chip.

Enter Atari. Or re-enter Atari.

Once Nintendo made games cool again, Atari wanted back in the market. Atari's programmers tried and failed to create a chip that could bypass the 10NES, so in the meantime Atari played ball and licensed some of the games in their catalogue for the NES. Because the company could only legally use its own name on arcade games, Atari created a subsidiary called Tengen and published under that name. Unlike other third party developers, Tengen was bringing some already-popular games to the table. Tengen asked Nintendo to waive the two-year exclusivity agreement and the five-game maximum. Nintendo held firm.

So Tengen put out three licensed games for the NES—*Pac-Man*, *Gauntlet*, and *R.B.I. Baseball*—and then got sneaky: They had their lawyers tell the U.S. Copyright Office that Nintendo was suing Tengen, and that Tengen needed to see the patent for the 10NES chip to prepare an adequate defense for the lawsuit. But once Tengen got the patent, they used the chip's specs to make a program called the Rabbit that bypassed the 10NES. Equipped with the Rabbit, Tengen began selling unlicensed versions of their games in any store that would have them.

Nintendo sued Tengen on the grounds that the Rabbit was a direct copy of the 10NES. Both sides settled, leaving Tengen free to try to sell its unlicensed games, but also leaving Nintendo free to lean on retailers to quit stocking Tengen games. Fearing Nintendo's wrath, most stores complied.

•

There was one other way to get around the 10NES chip.

In 1988—before Wisdom Tree, before *Bible Adventures*—tech consultant Dan Lawton was free-lancing in southern California, mostly working for a businessman named Eddy Lin.

Lawton was the son of novelist Harry Wilson Lawton, author of the novel *Willie Boy*, which was made into a Robert Redford movie, and the brother of screenwriter J.F. Lawton, who wrote the screenplays for *Pretty Woman*, *Under Siege*, and the Damon Wayans movie *Blankman*. But unlike his dad and brother, Dan Lawton's genius was for the technical.

One day Eddy Lin introduced Lawton to a Taiwanese businessman named James Chan. Chan showed Lawton a new way to get around the 10NES chip, one that didn't involve patent or copyright infringement: You zapped the 10NES chip with a voltage spike, disabling the chip for long enough to sneak past its defenses. Chan's simple solution to this complex problem was a bit like the famous scene in *Raiders of the Lost Ark* when a swordsman steps out and waves his sword expertly, challenging Indiana Jones to an epic battle, and Indy just shoots him.

Chan's use of a transistor/capacitor circuit was "a bit unreliable in its early form" according to Lawton, so Lawton took a couple of months and, with an oscilloscope and a screwdriver, reverse-engineered the NES and refined a circuit that reliably disabled the 10NES chip.

Lawton founded a new game company, Color Dreams, in the wake of this discovery. Eventually, each of Lawton's games featured a few seconds of what looks like a loading screen that says, "Starting Machine / Please Wait…" But the machine's not so much being started as overridden. Lawton could now make NES games without involving Nintendo at all.

Many people have mistakenly told the Color Dreams/ Wisdom Tree story as if Lawton and company were doing something firmly illegal. Instead, his company existed in a legal gray area. Theirs was a defensible position, but video games were such a new industry that if the tide were to shift in Nintendo's favor, Color Dreams would be sunk.

So why risk it? Why not play ball like LucasArts and everyone else?

Because Dan Lawton was not George Lucas, and playing ball took startup capital Lawton didn't have. "[Nintendo] charged us eleven dollars for each game cartridge, with a minimum purchase quantity and six months to deliver," Lawton said in an interview with NES World.[1] "We could produce them for three dollars, make just 100 [units] if we wanted to, and do it in two days. Nintendo had it all set up to drain all the money from companies and give them nothing in return. It was a really bad deal." To Lawton, going unlicensed was the only way the existence of his company was even possible.

Lawton partnered with his former client, Eddy Lin, and Eddy's brother Tom, got Taiwanese investors involved, and arranged to have the games' ROMs made in Taiwan by a chipmaker named UMC. In designing the plastic game cartridges, Eddy took care to avoid replicating the shape of licensed NES carts—Nintendo had a copyright on the cart design. Gone were the trademark ridges on the upper lefthand corner of each

---

1 Most of Color Dreams/Wisdom Tree developer interviews that I did not conduct myself are from two Nintendo fan sites, the Warp Zone (neswarpzone.com) and NES World (nesworld.com).

cart, and each game would come in baby blue instead of the except-for-*Zelda* gray of licensed NES carts.

Having found a way to work around Nintendo's tight standards, Color Dreams could now make any kind of games they wanted: no matter how sexy, violent, crass, political, or religious. Their only quality control check came from the invisible hand of the free market itself, a fickle and negligent god if there ever was one. Now all they needed was games.

AN ODD KIND OF
TECHNOLOGY

AFTER TEACHING MY AFTERNOON Composition class at a Catholic liberal arts college, I booked it from the west side of Los Angeles to a Santa Clarita Starbucks to meet Dan Burke. Three days earlier, I'd reached out to him over email and he replied within thirteen minutes asking when I wanted to meet.

I was nervous: Burke was one of Color Dreams's most important developers. And unlike most of his former colleagues, Burke remained in the video game industry for his entire career. During a tenure at Blizzard, he even worked on *Warcraft III* and *World of Warcraft*.

But when I arrived, Burke immediately put me at ease. A short friendly guy in glasses, t-shirt, and jeans, Burke looked young for his mid-40s. Quick to joke, going into voices and imitations frequently, and just as quick to state an opinion, Burke had a mind that was always going.

In the line to order our drinks, I told Burke how I first discovered Color Dreams, playing the copies of

Bible Adventures and *Joshua* I'd checked out at church. And when we sat with our coffees, my iPhone now recording us, Burke casually asked, "Are you still a Christian today?"

I hesitated. Was I going to be the journalist who skillfully redirects his question back onto the interviewee?

"It's complicated," I said. "I have a hard time really buying it. But I come out of a culture where a lot of my best friends are Christians and some members of my family are Christians. I never did a big disaffiliation but I can't own it either."

"You're a cultural Christian," Burke said.

"Yeah, I feel like: Jews have Reform Judaism [where shared culture is more important than belief] but I don't know that Christians get a thing like that."

"There's progressive Christians, I guess."

"But progressive Christians are still supposed to buy it…"

It's religion we began with, and religion we circled back to over and over in our two-and-a-half-hour conversation, but it never felt like a tangent. Belief was essential to the story of Burke's time at the company. It was his Christian faith that made Burke quit Color Dreams, and it was his time at Color Dreams that made Burke lose his faith altogether.

•

Dan Burke was a student at Saddleback College—
"Home of Rick Warren," he said, "who I can't stand."
While Burke was working as the staff artist for the
school newspaper, he met a writer named Leo Gilreath
who told Burke about a guy he'd met at an arcade who
was working on making Nintendo games. Burke was
skeptical ("I was like, 'yeah, right,' you know?"), but
agreed to meet the guy at Round Table Pizza.

"And this guy was a really bright young Chinese guy,
Frank Waung, working at Unisys at the time." Waung
told Burke about a new company called Color Dreams
that ran a cattle call for developers in the paper. Waung
had already attended an informational meeting about
the opportunity.

"When I showed up at the meeting," Waung told the
Warp Zone, "they told us, about 25 respondents, that
they have figured out a way to get around the [10NES]
chip, and therefore can make and sell NES games. We
were supposed to write a game and storyboard it for the
next meeting. We also had to find a partner who would
be doing the artwork for the game. After the meeting,
we all went our separate ways to come up with a game."

Few of the eager programmers in that room would
actually finish their games, Lawton later noted. "That's
always the hardest part of programming," he said in an
email to me. "Finishing things."

Burke was excited about the project. "It turned out
the company was legit, had real money. I had a job at
Sterling Art in Irvine, making $6.50 an hour, and I told

my boss about this opportunity. And he said, 'If you don't take this job, I'm gonna fire you.'"

So Burke and Waung began work on "Drug Czar," a futuristic action game starring Agent Shadow, the last uncorrupt cop on the force, who must single-handedly clean the streets of drug dealers.

It was a lot of work for the pair to handle, particularly since Waung kept his job at Unisys and they both were working on spec, unsure of when or if they would be paid. "When I came home at 5:00 p.m., Dan and I would work 'til 2:00 in the morning," Waung said. "To stay awake we used to drink two liters worth of Dr. Pepper or Mountain Dew every night. We piled up all the empty bottles on the porch and soon we had a collection."

For months in 1989, they worked out of Waung's house. Waung headed up the coding using a proprietary kit Color Dreams had supplied, Dan's friend Leo from the school paper did most of the writing, and Burke was in charge of the art and music. "[Waung and I] had so much stake in this that there was a lot of pressure," Burke said. "We didn't know if the money was real yet. We argued over every detail."

There were a lot of technical problems in the early going. "Coding the NES was not very straightforward," Waung said, "since everything had to be done in assembly[2] with a cross compiler. […] I think when I was

2   Assembly is a low-level programming language with no regard for user-friendliness. It's hardcore. The code looks incomprehensible to outsiders.

finally done after six months, I wrote close to 20,000 lines of assembly code."

When the deadline arrived, Waung and Burke delivered "Drug Czar" to Dan Lawton, and finally each got paid $10,000. According to Waung, "Dan [Burke] used the money to buy a new Korg M1 keyboard and down payment on his Civic while I bought another computer."

The game was pretty rough by Nintendo standards— blocky characters and weak controls—but for two guys with few resources who'd never made a game before, the finished product was a huge victory. Color Dreams released "Drug Czar" as *Raid 2020* (fearing the word "drug" would bother parents) and suddenly Waung and Burke were game developers. "It was cool," Burke said, "'cause they put our names on the box. I hadn't even moved out yet. I was still living at home. I was twenty."

Lawton brought Burke on full time, and soon Burke was making enough money to move into a place of his own. "They brought me back in to work for this crazy amount of money on a crazy schedule. Seven days a week, twelve hours a day, it said in my contract. And then the contract was $555 a day. I don't know about the legality of it—1:00 p.m. to 1:00 a.m., every day."

For a while, Lawton and Burke worked from Lawton's home. During this time, Burke created a new game, *Robodemons* (1990), almost entirely by himself. You play a warrior with a boomerang who jetpacks through space and Hell to defeat evil demon lord Kull, who has "created a machine to transplant the souls of demons into the bodies of robots." The game alternates between a jetpacking space shooter and a jump-'n-shoot sidescroller. It's much better than *Raid 2020*, and more impressive considering the tools Burke had to work with.

"I had to draw everything on graph paper," Burke told me. "Even animations." He then used an actual NES controller to draw graphics pixel by pixel: "Scroll over, go to a pixel, select your color (it was CGA palette), and put your color in. No keyboards, no mouse. All Nintendo controller. So literally, it was like a game unto itself." Think *Mario Paint*, but sparer, cruder, and less fun. "I'd get really quick at it—BAM, Ba-BAM—over and over."

"What was that called?" I asked.

Burke laughed. "Hell!"

•

Color Dreams moved out of Lawton's house, and the team soon grew to include Robert Bonifacio, Vance Kozik, Roger Deforest, Ken Beckett, and teen prodigy Jon Valesh, who according to Kozik was fourteen years old when he joined Color Dreams.

When Kozik was offered the job, he dropped his San Antonio job, girlfriend, and cat, and moved to Color Dreams's new two-room office in Tustin, CA. Kozik was originally brought on to supervise the development team, maintaining quality while keeping production on schedule.

His first gig was helping debug a game called *Pesterminator: The Western Exterminator* (1990) with Bonifacio. The property of an actual Anaheim-based pest control company, *Pesterminator* stars Kernel Kleanup, a black-and-white cartoon throwback in a suit, top hat, and (for some reason) sandals, who smashes colorful bugs with a tiny ineffectual mallet. You walk through a house hunting for bugs to smash, and if you swing and miss one, the bug ricochets nonsensically to another part of the room. When you've killed all the bugs, you go to some other house and do it again. "You'd be hard pressed to find a video game worse than *Pesterminator*," Kozik said.

As Kozik oversaw the project, he found his team to be unmanageable. "When I wrote up a long list and told my opinions to the programmers and artists," he said, "they wouldn't even turn to look at me." To his and everyone else's relief, Kozik was soon put in game design and worked alongside his colleagues instead of over them.

Around this time, Lawton met the artist Nina Stanley (then Nina Bender) at Diedrich Coffee where she worked. Like Lawton, Stanley came from a famous family—her dad was Owsley "Bear" Stanley, the sound engineer and LSD supplier for the Grateful Dead. His enormous LSD empire eventually landed him in a federal prison for a couple of years in the early 70s. To

Deadheads, his biggest contribution was the fact that he recorded tapes from the mixing board of many Grateful Dead shows, and his live bootlegs eventually spread as far as his drugs.

Lawton paid Nina Stanley $100 to design the Color Dreams logo. He was happy with her work, and brought her on as an artist, but she hated the nameless drawing system as much as Burke did. "It was awful," she told the Warp Zone. "I quit after a couple of weeks and went back to making cappuccinos."

But Ken Beckett soon developed Nindraw, a mouse-based system for the PC, and Lawton enticed Stanley to come back and try it. "By this time I was divorced and trying to support a small child, and the idea of making twice as much and not having to do retail anymore was very appealing!" Stanley said. "So I tried again, and it was actually kinda fun."

"The palettes were extremely limited," Stanley continued, "and we had only 256 character spaces (a character being an eight-by-eight-pixel square) for background and another equal space for all the sprites, for each level. It was certainly challenging, but since I didn't know any other computer graphics programs to 'spoil' me, I didn't know any different. It was kind of like a puzzle, to fit in as much as I could, and to use it most efficiently."

"It was amazing," Burke said of the switch to Nindraw. "Using a mouse to draw was unheard of. *'What sorcery is this?'* The color selection was a lot easier.

And it was a little scary too because the ceiling had gone way up. More was expected of you. It was like going from an 8-bit program to a 24-bit program."

Nina Stanley excelled within her limitations and "turned out to be a genius at producing video game graphics," according to Lawton. "Nina was especially good at making a few pixels look alive." Stanley signed on with Color Dreams full-time, and soon began to bring her son to all-night coding sessions. He'd play for a bit and then fall asleep under her desk.

•

The process of developing games at Color Dreams was, as Roger Deforest told me, "very casual." "If you had an idea," he said, "you'd blurt it out and the programmer might code it. Lawton would always interject with ideas on what he thought would make the games fun. It was his company, so we'd usually include his ideas."

Jon Valesh put it more bluntly: "We were left alone to sink or swim, and then second-guessed."

Other times, Valesh continued, requests were made on behalf of Color Dreams's Taiwanese investors. "A very popular in-joke [...] at the time was, 'You've got to add a pink elephant. Pink elephants are fun,' referring to the tendency of some of the managers/investors to make strange requests which were in no way based on gameplay or Western culture. The two final enemies in *Secret Storm* were a good example." *Operation Secret*

Storm (1991), an embarrassing half tongue-in-cheek, half authentically-xenophobic game about then-President George H.W. Bush singlehandedly fighting brown people in the Middle East, ends its semi-realistic one-man-army story with a battle against a series of nonspecific ghosts and then, at the end, a Saddam Hussein clone who can magically turn back and forth from a man into an airplane.

"I'd always have to deal with Tom Lin," Burke told me, and began to imitate Lin in an almost Australian-sounding accent, "*Ah, hi Dan. We need to change the Baby Boomah³ cover to be more blue.*" His brother, Eddy, meanwhile, "was famous for barging in with a terrible idea and then making us do it." *Raid 2020* was a mostly realistic crime-fighting game, and Eddy insisted that at the end the main hero be riding a bee, which Burke and Waung thought was ridiculous. "But [Eddy's] like, '*He's gotta be riding a bee, yeah.*' He would affirm his own ideas."

Sometimes the Lin brothers meddled with more than just the games. Eddy Lin once called Roger Deforest at work and fired him because his art was not "Japanese enough." There had been no buildup to the firing and Deforest was blindsided. That same day, Dan

---

3   Color Dreams's first released game, when not spoken in an accent, is called *Baby Boomer* (1989). You use your NES Zapper light gun to shoot dangerous creatures that are trying to kill a baby. It would not be their last game about trying to prevent a baby from dying violently.

Lawton took Deforest out to coffee and rehired him as a contractor to do the same work he'd just been doing.

The team took turns picking CDs or tapes to play while they worked. Deforest played N.W.A and Public Enemy, Burke played synthpop like Depeche Mode and Camouflage, and Kozik played The Ramones and Frank Zappa. "And for some reason," Deforest added, "Lawton was into L'Trimm's 'Cars With the Boom' so we heard that a million times."

Everyone made their own hours. While Valesh worked a normal day shift, Deforest says he and Burke would typically "stroll in at 4:00 p.m., draw some sprites, go get a late dinner with the other employees, BS with them for a couple of hours, play some levels of *Golden Axe*, and then go back to work." It was between BS and *Golden Axe* that Lawton sometimes took the team out to a strip club.

After work, the team would keep hanging out. Dan Lawton remembered, "We used to jump into Jim's convertible and head to Jim Meuer's house in the hills because he had a swimming pool." In the morning, Burke and Deforest would head back to their shared apartment and create synthpop on Burke's Korg M1. "He had all the fun toys," Deforest said. Deforest and Burke called their band The Phobics, and recorded an album called *Priest in Heat*.

All the goofing off was only possible because everyone worked such long hours. It was Lawton's own scrappy little two-room Google where your work was your life but your life was pretty fun. "Often times, we practically lived in [the office]," Kozik told the Warp Zone. "It wasn't uncommon to see Jim Treadway or Jon Valesh asleep in the oversized *Star Trek* swivel chairs."

Finishing games quickly was important to Color Dreams because sales were slow. Nintendo of America had muscled all the major retailers like Toys "R" Us and KB Toys out of selling unlicensed games. *If you sell their unlicensed games, we won't let you sell our licensed games,* Nintendo implied—or by some accounts, threatened outright. Nintendo even threatened legal action against any stores that sold Tengen games, which further soured the stores' relationships with unlicensed developers. Color Dreams instead sold their games through independent toy stores, video rental stores, and especially through mail-order catalogues.

What Color Dreams lacked in distribution they made up for in volume. "Sometimes we'd work 80 hours per week to finish something," Lawton said. "At one point we hired five artists in Mexico to draw games for us, but it turned out that an artist couldn't really do anything useful unless they worked closely with a programmer." So the team did most of the work in-house, kept their heads down, and made games as quickly as they could.

"We all made the best of what we had to work with, and had a good time doing it," Deforest told me. "It's funny that I mostly remember the people at Color Dreams more than I do the games."

Dan Lawton was the mad genius whose work made Color Dreams possible and the cool, older-brother-type boss who kept the team happy. He'd regularly buy donuts for the office and was very patient with his developers, even when they turned in sub-par work.

Today, Lawton describes his former management style as "too lax" and "kind of crazy," but he guesses that since all his employees were so young, "they just assumed it was normal." Still, the Color Dreams era was a happy time. "There were always lots of young people around," Lawton said. "I don't get along with older people. Young people find me amusing. Older people find me annoying and tend to bully me."

Lawton took it upon himself to expand the minds of his young employees. "Dan would expose me to a lot of new food because I was Mr. White-bread Orange County guy," Dan Burke told me. Other times, he simply allowed his staff a window into what Burke called Lawton's "very chaotic personal life." "He'd tell me the huge arguments he got into with his crazy girlfriends," Burke told me. One of these girlfriends was physically abusive, but Lawton took it in stride. "He was so passive," Burke said. "She was attacking him, and she was kind of a bigger woman. He would come back, like, [*casually surprised voice*] 'Look at my arms, Dan—she *scratched* me.'"

For a while, Lawton moved into a two-story house in Newport Beach with Kozik, Deforest, and their co-worker Jim Treadway. "Across the street [...] motorcycles would run around the parking lot at night, and very pretty young women in bikinis would watch," he told me. "I figured my handsome programmers would bring a lot of them into our beach house and I'd get to hang out with them too." In this sense, the experience was a letdown. "They were very young men, and young men tend to be awkward with women. No one ever has nearly as much fun when they are young as they think they should."

"Dan Lawton was like an intelligent big kid," Deforest remembered. "Always inquisitive. [...] He was sort of a day-dreamer, futurist, entrepreneur who was grounded in the present." When Lawton brewed his own beer, for instance, "he had an innocent, child-like fascination about it," Deforest said. "He was like that with all his projects. One day he decided he wanted to start building humanoid robots, bought a bunch of machinery, rented a warehouse, and just started making robots. I remember seeing a metal hand with movable fingers, but the wires weren't hooked up yet. I'm not sure he ever finished it."

"He's the kind of guy where whatever he's working on, that's his world," Burke said.

Today, Lawton describes himself with much less admiration than his former employees. "I was just autistic," Lawton told me. "But I didn't know that myself. It was sort of a new illness. The school system had tried to put me in the special needs classes when I was in the second grade. My mother made a big stink about it, and they gave me an IQ test. The result put me in the gifted classes instead [...] and my family forgot about it until I reached my 50s, when I figured it out myself."

Lawton also practiced transcendental meditation, and claimed to Deforest that he could float while in a trance. "I found that awfully suspicious!" Deforest told me. "I offered to videotape it while out of the room, and he said no."

Still, Lawton was a natural skeptic and enjoyed challenging his employees' beliefs—perhaps Dan Burke's most of all.

"I was a Christian back then," Burke told me over coffee. "My brother would make fun of me because I had a Precious Moments Bible. I had friends and fellowship. I understood the language of belief. I was raised Catholic but was more of a nondenominational Christian. I was voting Republican. I was a Rush Limbaugh fan. [...] But we would have these arguments that [Lawton] called How Many Angels Can Dance on the Head of a Pin arguments," Burke continued. "I would defend Christianity as a believer and he would attack it as a nonbeliever."

Lawton characterizes himself as something more complicated. "I was somewhat of a Bible hobbyist at the time," he said. "I studied all religious texts. [...] My father was an anthropologist who studied Indian culture at Morongo. I'd been in contact with the two sorcerers who lived there. [...] I didn't see any incompatibility between religions. To me they were all an odd kind of technology, something much older but not that different from computers."

As the religious debates continued, the rest of the office got into it too. "Jon Valesh was arguing on the atheist side," Burke said. "And he would be like, 'Dan, here's the thing. *If God created us, who created him?*'"

It was the problem of evil—the question of why a perfect God would allow the existence of evil—that most stumped Burke. "I'd go home and I would read my Bible, and it would make it worse. I'd have more questions."

•

In the Bible, most big ideas come directly from on high. It's God himself who tells Jonah to scold some wicked Ninevites, God himself who inspires Abraham to nearly murder his son, and God himself who through fire tells Moses to lead the Jews out of Egypt. He sends the angel Gabriel—my namesake—to tell Mary to get ready for a God-baby, and there's a literal flash of heavenly light when the voice of Jesus asks Saul-turned-Paul, "Why do you persecute me?" At Color Dreams, the big idea for Bible games came instead from a joke.

One day, Lawton said in jest to Nina Stanley that Color Dreams ought to "make a game with Jesus jumping around." The idea got a big laugh from the programmers. "Everyone knew that would create a terrible uproar," Lawton said, "maybe even ending in scandal in the news cycle."

"I really didn't mean anything offensive by it," Lawton explained. "I just found it interesting that people got so upset about their religious icons. Either your religion is true and you shouldn't be offended, or it isn't and you ought to pay more attention."

Over the following week, the joke began to turn serious. One of the programmers pointed out how well Christian music sold. Singers who could never make it outside the bubble thrived in the Christian market.

A plan to develop Bible games came together quickly. "Dan Lawton approached us programmers and told us the company was going to begin focusing on Christian-themed video games," Roger Deforest said. "Dan saw this as an untapped market, and he had a vision to turn famous stories from the Bible into games that children can have fun playing and learn scripture at the same time."

"They knew they had a guaranteed number of sales," Dan Burke said, "sorta like how the Republicans rely on the evangelical base."

Here's where the story begins to resemble "Christian Rock Hard," the *South Park* episode quoted in this book's epigraph. In the episode, Cartman bets his friends he can sell a million records before they can. To win the bet, he forms a Christian rock band called Faith + 1. "It's the easiest, crappiest music in the world, right?" Cartman reasons. "If we just play songs about how much we love Jesus, all the Christians will buy our crap!" When Kyle tells Cartman his idea is "retarded," Cartman replies, "It worked for Creed."

Not only were Christian games a new product for an eager demographic, the flourishing Christian bookstore market offered better distribution than Color Dreams had ever seen. Christian bookstores had never sold Nintendo games before, so there was nothing Nintendo could hold over them. "The Christian market was attractive because they didn't have any Nintendo games at all, and didn't give a fig about Japanese distribution," Lawton said. "In fact, if you told them that Nintendo might be angry about them selling our games, that made them want to sell them even more."

•

Color Dreams co-owner Eddy Lin initially hated the idea of Christian games, but came on board as he researched the size of what is now known as the Christian retail industry. "Eddy realized there was a database of 7,000 Christian stores who would love to sell the games," Lawton said. "One thing Eddy could do best was take a phone database, and manage sales people to call all the numbers and sell product."

Christian bookstores were a cultural force that had been growing ever since 1950, the year the Christian Booksellers Association (CBA) was formed. Of course, bookstores with a Christian emphasis had existed before this time, but the border between a regular bookstore and a Christian one was more porous. It was the CBA that made the Christian bookstore a movement. These booksellers saw their work as a form of "retail ministry," and often offered in-store Bible studies, concerts, readings, and prayer groups. "We talked with seekers, prayed with those who were hurting, did impromptu counseling, and hosted midnight music parties and pastors' breakfasts," writes Christian bookseller Cindy Crosby of her experience running a store in the 80s and 90s. "Our staff members were encouraged to drop what they were doing if someone needed to talk."

The industry expanded steadily throughout the 60s, 70s, and 80s. In the early days, the stores devoted most of their shelf space to meaty theological books with only ten percent reserved for Church supplies. Over time, the stores' selection tilted more mainstream and featured—like the retail megastores with which the Christian bookstores competed—a lot more than just books. For this reason, the CBA changed its name to the Association for Christian Retail and began to stock Christian posters, toys, jewelry, doodads, picture frames, and bumper stickers. To call most of these items inessential would be an understatement—once word got out that Christians liked Christian shit, retailers began to create Christian everything.

As a believer, Dan Burke had a big problem with pandering to a market of his fellow Christians. "I was annoyed at the fact that they were doing Bible games," he said. "I didn't want to sully the Lord's name by making profit. Jesus did not like the money-changers."

I asked Burke what Lawton thought about the prospect of making Bible games. "He was very pragmatic," Burke said. "He was the type to be like, *'Well there's money to be made. Let's make some money. Come on, guys.'*"

With that promise of money, a new game studio was born. And as with Paul on the road to Damascus, a newly Christian studio required a new name.

•

Wisdom Tree.

The name sounds wholesome, natural, and evokes a sweet children's book by Shel Silverstein. But it also appears to directly reference a Bible story in which Adam and Eve eat from a tree so that they may, as a talking snake puts it, "be like God." According to the book of Genesis, the Wisdom Tree was the source of all our troubles—the reason we've got to work jobs instead of taking turns going down on each other in a lush equatorial garden. For a company looking to win the trust of Christians, the name is an interesting choice.

But I doubt most people are as likely to overthink the point as I am.

To distance their new Christian games from their previous secular offerings, Wisdom Tree ordered new black carts to replace Color Dreams's distinct baby blue ones.[4]

The new company also required a new sales team.

Brenda Huff worked at Christian book publisher Gospel Light Publications in Ventura, CA until her husband's promotion relocated them to the Brea area east of Los Angeles. "I decided to look for work after January 1, 1991," she told me in an email. "On January 2, I checked the want ads and Wisdom Tree had an ad in the paper for sales associates with Bible knowledge." Huff went in for an interview and was hired on the spot.

New hires made up the majority of Wisdom Tree's sales team, as Color Dreams hadn't previously had the demand to require a sales team. A young pastor named Michael Wilson had been named a vice president at Wisdom Tree, and Huff worked directly under him.

Huff began in phone sales, pitching Wisdom Tree's forthcoming games to the Christian bookstores, but her bosses soon realized that her work with Gospel Light made her a huge asset. "The other four reps hired had Bible college degrees," Huff said. "I was the only one

---

4   Their first game, however, would come in both colors, since there were still so many blue carts left in inventory.

with experience in the [Christian retail] market. I also came with a pretty good customer list to start."

Huff was made sales supervisor and put in charge of sales, marketing, and trade shows, where she focused, with much success, on the Christian retail industry, including accounts with Evangelical behemoths like James Dobson's ultraconservative media company, Focus on the Family (FOTF)—a company that later became famous for its ex-gay ministry, Love Won Out, and for Dobson's role in getting George W. Bush elected president.

Office culture changed as Wisdom Tree grew. Huff remembers the offices for their camaraderie, their great Halloween parties, and their multiculturalism: "Caucasian, Hispanic, African American, Taiwanese, and Programmers. Yes they are a nationality all to themselves. LOL!" What didn't change was that most of the development team remained on an opposite schedule of the sales team, wandering in around 3:00 in the afternoon and working through the night.

That wasn't the only difference between the development team and the sales team. "[Michael Wilson] managed his sales team like a ministry, and even had prayer sessions in the conference room," said Lawton. "He had a few raggedy people on his sales team, some of which must have recently come to Christianity because of a crisis in their life. I remember one young woman who had bandages on her wrists for a while, and they were bleeding in what looked like the result of a horizontal cut. Another had a serious mood disorder. But Michael rallied them together, and even had contests involving popping balloons with notes specifying a prize inside, and a little fishing pond where you hooked a fish with a prize note in its mouth. The person with the best sales for the week got to fish or pop a balloon."

Still, the development schedule at Wisdom Tree was far more demanding than in the Color Dreams days. "The company grew to over 60 employees (mainly sales and production) and game design became very businesslike," Vance Kozik told the Warp Zone. "Schedules were enforced, and the design/graphics team was very small compared to the Bunch Games[5]/ Color Dreams days. Now when programmers slept at the office, it was because of deadlines."

To Huff, this confluence of talent was too perfect to be a coincidence. "How do you suppose such a vastly diverse group of people were at the right place, at the right time to produce the only Bible-based cartridge arcade style games?" asked Huff in an NES World interview. "Being one of the born-again Christians mentioned in many of [NES World's] articles, I have my own ideas on the matter." Was it possible that creating these games had been God's plan for these godless heathen developers all along?

---

5   Color Dreams briefly tried selling games like *Mission Cobra* and *Galactic Crusader* under the label Bunch Games. None of the games were made in-house and all performed poorly.

To Dan Burke, the answer was no.

Color Dreams began developing games almost exclusively as Wisdom Tree just as Dan Burke arrived at his solution to the problem of evil: There was no God.

Apostasy stories always drum up an anxiety in me that runs even deeper than the already daunting Fear of Hell: When I was fourteen, my mom decided (or admitted to herself) that she didn't believe in God and divorced my dad the preacher. When my dad explained the situation to his entire congregation one Sunday morning, my mom's private decision became a community discussion—one that made my sister and me deeply uncomfortable. When I hear stories like Dan's wholesale disavowal of Christianity, an illogical part of me assumes it comes with years of personal, family, and professional struggle. I stop just short of asking, "How did you *survive* it?" That's my baggage, not Dan's.

"Literally, a month [after my conversations with Lawton began], I was an atheist," he said. "Not 30 years, not fifteen years—I was like, 'Okay, I'm wrong.' Because I knew that I was beaten in the argument. And I was intellectually honest enough to understand that I had lost these points. But I couldn't defend it. It's like defending O.J. [Simpson]—who did it, by the way. He absolutely did it."

So when he was a Christian, Burke didn't want to work on Bible games that trivialized his faith. "And then when I was an atheist," he said, "I didn't want to do Bible games because I was an atheist. I was like, 'I'm not working on that crap. I don't believe in that stuff.' So I was screwed."

Burke was the only atheist on the team who had an ethical problem creating Bible games. So what was the harm, I asked Burke, in making Christian games with his atheist friends?

He didn't have one answer for me, he had several. "Believing in something that isn't true makes you do things based on that belief. [...] If you go stab a dog in the eye and then ask for forgiveness—if you really believe that Jesus died for your sins, you're forgiven. And that to me is unethical. Waste of time. Waste of money. And the Bible's been used as justification for a lot of bad behavior: fighting women's suffrage, fighting choice, fighting birth control. Entire third world countries don't have sufficient birth control because they're under the thumb of the Pope. Believing that a God will send you to Hell for failing a test of faith It knows the answer to. Shame."

Before it could begin, Dan Burke's time at Wisdom Tree was finished.

BIBLE ADVENTURES

SET UP IN CHRISTIAN BOOKSTORES across the country were three-foot video displays introducing Wisdom Tree's 1990 debut, *Bible Adventures*, to the world. "This game promotes Bible literacy and teaches children about the Bible while they play a fun and exciting *Super Mario Bros.*-style video game," says a calm announcer as scenes from the game play onscreen.

A game about three Old Testament Bible characters each working on behalf of God himself, *Bible Adventures* is at once a single game and a bundle of three very similar platformers.

In the first and best-remembered of these games, "Noah's Ark," you play as an old white-bearded Noah with Hulk strength who must catch two of every species of animal so they can repopulate the Earth after the flood.

But you don't *lead* a horse to the ark. You pick the horse up and hold it above your head, like a champion, without threat of the horse breaking your back or even your stride. Roger Deforest told me, "We were playing *Super Mario Bros. 2* a lot at the time of making *Bible Adventures*," and it shows.

The animals, you soon discover, are stackable: While already carrying a horse, you can hoist another horse onto your pile—then a monkey, then a ram, then a couple of cows. Sure they'll all fall off the pile if you get hit—one of the game's less endearing mechanics—but it's fun while you've got them.

"Noah had to collect the animals," Deforest explained, "so someone came up with the idea of him actually picking up the animals and carrying them to the ark. I remember when we first showed this feature to Dan [Lawton], he was laughing like a little kid and couldn't stop. I had never seen him laugh so hard. We had a lot of fun putting *Bible Adventures* together. We had to rein ourselves in for fear of being too silly."

In the first stage, the animals are pretty compliant: The pigs are slippery until you feed them hay, the oxen fall out of your hands whenever you jump, and the monkeys must be bribed with bananas, but there are few dangers to make the job challenging.

In the second stage, snakes are everywhere, birds of prey dive at you, and the birds you want to capture fly away as you approach them. Violence becomes increasingly necessary. Whereas level one's pigs need to eat a bale of hay to be distracted, level two's pandas need to be knocked unconscious by the same bale.

The game's weak animal detection means that if an animal you're after goes offscreen, even briefly, it has probably disappeared and returned to its starting position. This is particularly annoying if you're about to return a stack of three animals to the ark and an eagle dive-bombs you, makes you drop all but the dumb turtle, and carries you in its talons to the top of the level. Or when a cornered raccoon jumps from his tree branch down to the forest floor, which is just out of view, and vanishes.

By stage three, the animal collection biz has gotten rote—particularly the routine of watching the animals enter the ark each time you drop them off, then again as you make your way through the checklist at the end of each level.

The goal soon switches and you are tasked with collecting seven of each type of food so the animals can survive the long trip ahead, but by then the "Noah's Ark" game has worn out its welcome and it's time to move on to one of the others.

While I remember the *Bible Adventures* of my youth as an "easy" game, I now see that it was only easy in that I felt the freedom to give up when I got bored.

•

The title screen of *Bible Adventures* plays Bach's "Jesu, Joy of Man's Desiring," best known as the song that is played while the bridesmaids, groomsmen, parents, and grandparents walk down the aisle at the beginning of a wedding. (It's also the basis for The Beach Boys' "Lady Linda.") Part of a larger twenty-minute cantata, our culture has plucked "Jesu" from its larger context and set it on repeat, much like the snippet Timbaland plucked from Egyptian composer Baligh Hamdi's song "Khosara Khosara" for Jay-Z's "Big Pimpin'." In both cases, the larger context is brilliantly jettisoned for the sweetest, most repeatable bars.

Naturally, we also do this with the Bible. Growing up, I was often told that you can't just *pick and choose* which parts of the Bible you want to believe—it's all or nothing. But every preacher, parent, picture book publisher, and Christian game developer must at least decide which Christian stories they want to highlight, just as all God-fearing Christians walk around with different versions of the Good Book in their heads, each impression distorted by the believer's tastes, interpretations, and imperfect memory.

For instance, there are 150 psalms in the psalter, but only one of them is a smash hit: 23. It's upbeat, it's optimistic, and it's got a strong central metaphor established by the first line, "The Lord is my shepherd," which gets developed throughout with images of pasture, waters, rod, and staff. Sure the metaphor falls apart at the end, but only so the writer can speculate that thanks to God, everything is going to be awesome forever.

According to Steve Knopper's *New York Times* article about the songwriter Sia, the music industry calls Psalm 23's ilk *high concept songwriting*—"coming up with a word or phrase that works as a simple, poignant, bankable metaphor, like the Katy Perry song 'Firework.'"

But much more often than its prayers, the Bible's biggest hits are its little self-contained anecdotes, myths, and parables. Adam and Eve. The Flood. The Burning Bush. The Parting of the Red Sea. The Ten Commandments. David and Goliath. Daniel in the Lion's Den. Jonah and the Whale. Lot's Tough Lot. Jesus in the Manger. Water into Wine. The Sermon on the Mount. The Prodigal Son. The Crucifixion. Paul's Conversion. The Apocalypse.

In choosing which stories to depict, Wisdom Tree, like all of us, took a Greatest Hits approach to the Bible. However, their sense of what the hits were took them in some surprising directions.

•

While Noah's Ark is one of the Bible stories you'd first nominate for a game called *Bible Adventures*, "Baby Moses" offers a less predictable premise: a mother defending her child from danger.

Moses's mom (or "a Levite woman" as the Bible calls her) is the star of this game, and it's her job to get Baby Moses to the Nile so that she can float her son downriver in a basket. This mission would be more understandable if the Nile was not in the foreground of the first frame of the first level and was not in nearly every frame for the entire rest of the game. But Moses's mom is a picky Levite and she wants to abandon her baby where she wants.

She also wants to *hold* her baby how she wants: Basically, she just *Super Mario 2*'s the baby over her head like it's an engorged vegetable, a Birdo egg, or a subdued Shyguy, and impressively holds the baby aloft like that indefinitely. Even while running at up to 10 mph.

That is, unless she throws Baby Moses across the screen, which is what the B button in this Bible Game for Children is for—hurling your baby mightily across the desert and hoping for the best.

In a different kind of game, this option could be strategic: You might be asked to throw the baby across a gorge to be able to cross it at all, or to place Baby Moses on a switch so that you can unlock a necessary door, or to use Baby Moses as a miraculously powerful weapon that kills any pushy Egyptian he encounters. *Bible Adventures* affords none of these opportunities or challenges; in fact, "Baby Moses" offers no method to fight back against your attackers at all.[6] It is therefore never a good idea to throw Baby Moses.

The reason, then, that you are able to throw your child is simple: All the characters in *Bible Adventures* have the same controls—elderly Noah, buff young David, and our Levite Woman—and the buttons for each Adventure do the same thing: run, jump, pick up, and throw. Wisdom

6   This gameplay feature might seem to imply that Wisdom Tree intentionally promotes a radical Christ-like pacifism, but this impression will soon be undone.

Tree could have programmed each of the three games to have different controls based on the needs of each game, but it would have taken more work.

•

While "Noah" is the nostalgic favorite of most people I've talked to (or at least the game they remember most vividly), "Baby Moses" is the *Bible Adventures* game most popular in the community of speedrunners—players who attempt to beat games as quickly as possible, often exploiting a game's code in surprising ways. Today the biannual speedrunner Olympics are Awesome Games Done Quick (AGDQ) and Summer Games Done Quick (SGDQ), live charity speedrun marathons that stream online and are archived on YouTube.

"Baby Moses" world record-holder Brian Lee Cook (who speedruns as Brossentia, a reference to his sister's speedrunner name, Essentia) ran the game at SGDQ in 2013, and his performance offers an interesting glimpse into the bizarre mechanics of *Bible Adventures*. "I don't know how many times I'll die," he warns his audience before starting, "just because the physics are a little iffy." From behind him, another guy goes, "A *little*?"

When I reached out to Cook to see what I could learn about *Bible Adventures* from someone who knows it so intimately, he explained that speedrunning *Bible Adventures* is part of a newish tradition in speedrunning known as the "bad game scene," which began when Cook and fellow speedrunner Dragondarch challenged one another at *Athena* for the NES and *The Wizard of Oz* for the Super NES. "There is something special about bad games," Cook told me over email. "You have the chance to play through something that people set aside after a few minutes. […] Becoming a master of a terrible game is perfecting the imperfect, finding harmony within chaos, and bringing about a level of completeness to something held together with digital string."

In his "Baby Moses" run, Cook stays as low and as close to the river as possible, employing tiny bunny hops when necessary. This helps him overcome what he calls the designer's "unintended obstacles": "Most inputs in the game are extremely delayed, and because of that, you often end up trying to jump but end up doing short, repetitive hops that inevitably get you killed. Also, the character being played moves once every two or three frames rather than on each frame, causing problems with consistency." Many of his strategies reflect a necessary economy of movements: The fewer commands you give the game, the less likely the game is to screw something up.

At the beginning of the third stage, Cook turns this lag into an advantage: He picks up Moses, immediately falls through the floor, past the river, and runs along the bottom of the screen for the rest of the level, avoiding all danger. "As it turns out," Cook told me, "the world keeps moving on the frames where the character is still. Because of this, you can end up standing in the air for a couple of frames before entering the falling animation. If you do this and pick up Baby Moses while standing in the air, you'll fall while picking him up. For some reason, women picking up babies are invincible in Egypt, so you end up going through the river with no problem."

Mostly, though, Moses is much tougher than his mommy—so tough he lacks a health meter. Spiders that kill you will walk right past him. When you encounter a bird, the bird picks you up and carries you to the top of the screen while Moses waits for you on the ground. When a man appears from beneath a secret trapdoor and throws a gold bar at you, you drop an untroubled Moses to the ground. His only true predator is one of the many loinclothed Egyptian guards. When a guard sees you, he stabs you, makes you drop your baby, then picks up Moses and throws him into the Nile, where Moses drowns immediately.

Then, horrifically, the game keeps going. You don't die of sorrow. The guard doesn't taunt you. You just continue on to the end of the level, where you are greeted with the perversely understanding message, "Good work, but you forgot Baby Moses."

The game doesn't make this obvious, but there is one other way to deal with your son's death. If instead of continuing on, you mourn your way back to the beginning of the level… there's Baby Moses waiting for you, alive, unmoving, untroubled—The Boy Who Lived.

But since there are infinite continues in *Bible Adventures*, it's usually fastest to just kill yourself and start over.

•

"So how were the plots of these Bible games decided," I asked Burke, "amongst a crowd of atheist and agnostic game developers?"

"It was like doing a game about Cthulhu," he said. "What's the Cthulhu lore? They would just crack open the Bible and there was your story. Noah's Ark. There's a story right there."

The team took a similar approach to the games' music. One day, Lawton brought in a hymnal and had Deforest pick out whatever hymns he wanted to code. "Each note had to be programmed," Deforest explained. "I'd have the sheet music of some Christian song, and each note I'd have to transpose into a program. So when you played it, it'd go 'DOOT DEET DOOT DEET, DEET DOOT DEET DOOT…'" This is how "Jesu" wound up in the title screen of *Bible Adventures*.

"I did a lot of the design on *Bible Adventures* 'cause I was the only one in the group who had ever read the Bible," Nina Stanley told NES World. "After that, we hired some fundamentalist Christian types for the sales department, but in development, all the programmers were atheists, agnostics, or whatever, and I'm Catholic (which some of the sales guys didn't really think of as Christian!). Oh, and [Lawton] was Buddhist or something."

It was Eddy Lin who had the good sense to hire a sales team full of Christians who could not only talk the talk with Christian bookstores but could also offer Christian input on the games themselves. Lin had little understanding of Christianity and his own suggestions were less helpful. According to Lawton, Lin wanted to print a t-shirt that read, "Grab your joystick, here comes Moses!"

"I had to talk him out of that one," Lawton said.

•

The third and final *Bible Adventures* game, "David and Goliath," despite its promising name, is a game about collecting sheep and putting them in their designated area: a less-appealing retread of "Noah's Ark" bundled right in the game alongside "Noah's Ark" itself.

Your job is to collect four sheep in each of four levels as lions, scorpions, and rams attack you. The game's simple soundtrack plucks along, harp-like, as you navigate aggressively green landscapes.

The exception to the greenery is level three, which sets blue and gray stones against a black backdrop—it is a rare moment in *Bible Adventures* where color composition has clearly been considered. Level three's emphasis on a cramped horizontal space sets it apart from the other levels in every way, allowing for your enemies to pose a true threat to both you and each other. In the rightmost corner of this stage, I watched a lion savagely and continuously claw at his fellow lion (despite nearby sheep and rams to attack), a trail of *ZZZ*s reminding us that the attacked lion is not dead but merely sleeping.

As in "Baby Moses," you can often run right past many enemies without getting hit. Brian Lee Cook notes that this is especially true in early levels. "The more you play the game, the more you know which enemies you can run through without getting hit. As long as you get to the same place the same way, enemies will always behave the same." So while there may not be an internal logic to your enemies' actions, there is at least some consistency.

Not so in the fifth and final stage, which flips the script on the whole game. You are finally given a sling and stones that can slay enemy soldiers in a single hit, but the soldiers are not the problem: The game now demands you scale a mountain using timed jumps with janky controls while boulders fall on you. Whenever one of these boulders strikes you, you fall to the platform below, and if that platform holds a scorpion, you're doomed to fall again.

When Cook attempted a "David and Goliath" speedrun at 2014's SGDQ, he made the climb look easy, but later confided that the run had been "a miracle." "Those boulders are random. Pure random. […] The game hates anyone who plays the last level and pulls out all the stops to make them wish the Philistine had come to smash David quickly and quietly."

At the top of this mountain is Goliath's shield-bearer, whom you must knock off the cliff before Goliath will appear. Then, finally, you are treated to the legendary titular battle with Goliath himself. The boss's chief form of attack is to run at you, and you must hang back, jumping and tossing in such a way that your rock will strike his absurdly tiny hit box in just the right spot. It takes most players many tries.

I know this from YouTube and conversation, not from experience—I always get stuck attempting to jump past all those boulders.

The slapdash design of the game's painful conclusion reminds me of something Dan Burke told me when I met him for coffee: "One of the strategies of Color Dreams was just to get something out there before they got shut down."

So much of *Bible Adventures* conjures the image of a developer coding on deadline whose only edict is to keep from offending as best he can—to create a game a parent could squint at and go, "Yeah, that looks about right."

The Bible is merely a backdrop. The Adventure is often a slog. *Bible Adventures* is a game for no one.

•

It'd be tempting to leave it at that.

After all, hating on Wisdom Tree games has become a popular internet pastime among Christians and heathens alike.

Bible Adventures appears on two of Sean Patrick "Seanbaby" Reiley's worst games lists. "All the fun of learning about God with all the excitement of wandering around aimlessly," he writes in Cracked's "The 20 Worst NES Games of All Time" list. Even more damning is its inclusion in his "The 20 Worst Games [On Any Platform] Ever" list, sandwiched between *Extreme Sports with Berenstain Bears* and *Kris Kross: Make My Video*. The stigma has stuck to *Bible Adventures* pretty securely. "This game is notorious for being one of the worst, *worst* games for the NES system," says gamer Dan Seibert in a May 2014 *Bible Adventures* YouTube playthrough. He says it casually—it's simply common knowledge he's passing along.

"If Wisdom Tree were founded by people that were Christians that had an honest passion for video games, the games would be awesome!" writes Christian blogger CTrax of the blog Kingdom9. "But it's a company that was founded to provide a 'Christian alternative' to everything else."

But there's a disconnect between how these games are talked about now and how they were received when they were first released. While the internet is hard on *Bible Adventures*, it's largely because we forget how shitty the lion's share of NES games actually were—or we never played many of the bad ones in the first place. Most of my friends owned a copy of *Super Mario Bros. 3*. None of us owned *Draw a Dinosaur*.

And while today I'm frustrated by trying to catch birds in "Noah," avoid spiders in "Moses," and scale the mountain in "David," it never bothered me much as a kid. I merely played each game until it got so hard that I was bored—same as *Kung Fu*, same as *Donkey Kong*. Games were hard. What could you do?

Customers at the time received *Bible Adventures* fairly well. "Everyone I've talked to who played Wisdom Tree games really enjoyed them for at least trying to do something different and reach a niche audience," Deforest told me. "In fact, I remember reading the *Bible Adventures* feedback cards that the consumers sent back to us, and they were all very positive."

When I mentioned the disparity between the game's popularity in 1991 and its current bad reputation in an email to writer Michael P. Williams, he replied, "I wouldn't be surprised if some [internet] snark was reserved for the games simply because they were Christian. American popular culture has a strange relationship with domestic religion, and Americans themselves have weird relationships with majority cultures. I wonder if Americans would have been more receptive to a game like *Shinto Warriors!* or *Heroes of Zen: Adventures of Ikkyū* simply because they would be foreign and 'cool.'"

Even nonreligious games can be branded uncool if an aspect of it appears Christian. When in 1992 Taito/Takeru released their platformer *Lickle: Legend of the Holy Bell* in the United States, they gave it the accidentally biblical name *Little Samson*. In his YouTube series *The Gaming Historian*, Norman Caruso speculates that it's likely "many thought *Little Samson* was a religious game" and steered clear. And though it now retails $200+ as a paragon of early platforming, *Samson* flopped on release.

In 2014, Darren Aronofsky came out with a movie called *Noah* that was loosely based on the Bible story, which then became the subject of a familiar spat. Christians were up in arms before the movie's release because of Aronofsky's atheism, and the fact that he presented Noah as a brooding and potentially crazed servant of God. On Facebook, a former student of mine called *Noah* a "steaming pile of heretical horse manure," denouncing (his quotes) "Christian leaders" who recommended it. The film's idiosyncrasy and irreverence didn't stop its promotional campaign from pitching it to Christians as inspirational pap. "You stand alone and defy me?" a bad guy says to Russell Crowe's handsome, tortured take on Noah. Crowe pauses dramatically. "I'm not alone." The whole enterprise, as marketed to mainstream America, seemed vaguely embarrassing.

Whether you're a Christian or not, Christianity is the mass culture we Westerners are all swimming in. The Noah myth is so embedded in us, it's uncomfortable to see a game or film that portrays it explicitly.

I once heard somewhere that a religion has to be dead (or dead to you) for you to really be able to see the beauty in it. I like the idea of people reading the Bible as a beautiful mystery instead of a textbook, loving it the way I loved the Greek myths for a couple months in fourth grade.

•

As Imagine Dragons, Tyler Perry, and *Bible Adventures* remind us, sometimes things that are easy to make fun of nonetheless make a boatload of money.

Although we don't know exactly how many copies of *Bible Adventures* were sold when accounting for the eventual Sega Genesis and Game Boy ports, the most common figure reported is 350,000.

Sure 350,000 is no *Thriller*, but remember that Wisdom Tree achieved its success with only the support of Christian bookstores and their related catalogues, and that the majority of licensed Nintendo games did not sell nearly as well. It may go without saying that *Bible Adventures* sold far better than any of Color Dreams's previous titles too.

In the press, though, the success story was simply offered up as a curiosity.

"Move over, Mario," begins an *Orlando Sentinel* fluff piece from March of 1991.

"Move over, Mario Brothers," begin a *Newport News* article from that same December.[7]

---

7   This isn't direct plagiarism so much as a couple of examples of journalism's weird yen for the expressions, "Move over, X," and "Step aside, Y." A cursory googling of "Move over, Mario" yields 107,000 results.

When I asked Roger Deforest over email if he or anyone else on the development team ever had to pretend to be more Christian than they were, it was kind of a dumb question. This was before the internet, before the boom of games journalism, before anyone would ask a developer about his process—let alone his deeply held spiritual beliefs. "Nobody knew who we were," he replied, "so there was no need to pretend."

In fact, none of the articles about *Bible Adventures* mention Color Dreams whatsoever, which was how Wisdom Tree wanted it. No need to muddy an inspirational title with the mention of a vaguely blasphemous past release like *Robodemons*.

All of the news articles from this era instead portray Wisdom Tree as a new and thoroughly Christian enterprise, and extensively quote Wisdom Tree VP Michael Wilson, the newly hired pastor who ran the sales team. "I just wanted to develop something that was adventuresome as well as exciting," he told the *Sentinel*, "but at the same time had a lot of different moral issues that could pretty much mold [a player's] personality."

Wilson was Wisdom Tree's perfect public face for how completely he seemed to believe in the company's mission. "Third-graders on an average spend 900 hours in the classroom but 1,100 hours in front of the Nintendo," Wilson says. "If they're watching things that are negative, it can be damaging." The *Orlando Sentinel* article concludes, "But [Wilson] says the company is out for more than video business. 'We don't look at it as competing,' Wilson said. 'We look at it as a form of ministry.'"

Christian bookstores reported strong sales—"We can hardly keep them in," says one owner in the *Newport News*—and extolled the games' virtues. "Most video games are violent, have hypnotic music, and involve witchcraft of wizardry," says Ed Schultz, manager of Beardsley's Bible and Books, in the *Lodi News-Sentinel* in December 1991. "These are based on Bible stories." Schultz might've been surprised to learn that Wisdom Tree games would eventually contain every item on his shit list—especially *Joshua*, a game where you kill wizards with the power of hypnotic music.

When our dutiful reporters called upon Nintendo for comment, Nintendo chose to feign ignorance of Wisdom Tree's entire operation, casting themselves as the cruiseliner who doesn't have time to notice little skiffs like Wisdom Tree. "They've told me they don't even know of [*Bible Adventures*]," said Ruby Barcklay of a PR firm that represented Nintendo.

"Once we started making Christian games, they started to think twice about hassling us more," Lawton confirmed. "Besides having the feeling that Christianity is an odd belief system, the Japanese also know that this irrational thinking produces a lot of emotions in the people who believe in it. I suspect they were a little afraid of bad publicity. And since they didn't make religious games, maybe it was okay for us to specialize in that area."[8]

In other words, Nintendo was sitting this fight out. As Stephen L. Kent puts it in *The Ultimate History of Video Games*, Nintendo knew better than to go "after a tiny company that published innocuous religious games." He concludes, "Ignoring Wisdom Tree was the only logical course of action."

However, Wisdom Tree was not finished disrupting Nintendo's monopoly. Determined not to become a one-hit wonder, the company was already at work on its follow-ups to *Bible Adventures*. And for inspiration, they turned to both the Bible itself and their own back catalogue.

---

8   According to Lawton, Nintendo later cited Wisdom Tree when suing other unlicensed game studios: "They would point to us as having done it the right way, successfully, to reduce the likelihood a judge would consider antitrust arguments."

MINING FOR TREASURE

ONE TIME, JESUS WAS HEADING FOR JERUSALEM and a rich guy allegedly asked Jesus what he, the rich guy, ought to do if he wanted to live forever. Jesus mentioned the commandments about honesty, peacefulness, and honoring parents. *Right, but what else?* the rich guy wanted to know. Jesus suggested the guy sell everything he had, give it to the poor, then join the crowd of people who had lately been following Jesus around. The rich guy didn't want to, and left.

My guess is this encounter bummed out everyone present: the rich guy, Jesus's cohort, and of course Jesus himself, the type of leader whose eyes glazed over whenever conversation got too legalistic or transactional. Sick of questions like, "How many good deeds + prayers + sins avoided + conversions = fun-filled eternity?" Jesus always seemed to want to be asked, "Teacher, what's an awesome thing I could spend my time doing?"

For this reason, the alliance between Christianity and commerce has always been fragile.

At the Council of Clermont in 1095, Pope Urban II kicked off the Church's first Muslim-killing Crusade with the good news that all crusaders who'd confessed their sins would get a free pass to the afterlife.

In the 1500s, the Catholic Church schemed up the concept of indulgences, where you could pay the Church and they'd officially take time off your cleansing stay in the fires of Purgatory. You still had to go to confession to keep yourself out of Hell, but if you had the cash, indulgences were a great way to fastpass yourself through Heaven's waiting room.

However, it was hard to tell what the rules were and who was authorizing them. Documents got forged; dudes faked piety. Professional fundraisers called pardoners used indulgences to kickstart church projects, and got carried away with their promises about what kind of rewards a high-tier backer could expect. More recently, the Church has been offering indulgences for community volunteering, participation in World Youth Day, and following Pope Francis on Twitter. (His English-language account is at 5.48 million followers last I checked—decent, though no Rihanna.)

The practice was market-driven enough that in 1517 Martin Luther suspected that the Church had taken a couple of steps away from God's best interests, and he eventually wrote a 95-point disputation all about it, posting his manuscript on the door of the Castle Church of Wittenberg. A lot of people got on board with Luther after the printing pressers disseminated his writings, and the Protestant Church became Pepsi to the Catholic Church's Coke.

In the late 20th century, Protestants began to dream of a Christian culture apart from all the secular abortions and violent orgies, and sought to bring about a separatist Christian culture—chiefly through commerce. Christians kept singing that popular 60s hymn, "They'll Know We Are Christians By Our Love," but knew in their hearts that a bumper sticker was both easier and more direct, broadcasting faith from the parking lot while practitioners strolled Target in peace.

And so there appeared Christian apocalypse novels, Christian detective thrillers, Christian sci-fi and fantasy, Christian stuffed animals, Christian vegetable cartoons, Christian cookbooks, Christian Bible-based diets, Christian death metal, Christian ska/punk (of which thirteen-year-old Gabe Durham was a big, big fan), Christian skateboarding videos, DVDs about a family of backcountry Christian duck hunters, Christian films starring Kirk Cameron, Christian manicure sets, Christian hand and body cream, Christian rings symbolizing sexual self-denial that churches asked young women (but never young men) to wear at all times, Christian Bible verse t-shirts whose designs riffed on the marketing campaigns of global brands, and—it was only a matter of when—Christian video games.

Several fundamentalist Muslims flew planes into three American buildings. We asked "why?" and were told it was because they hated our faith and freedoms. We asked how we could help and we were told to shop.

•

In Ken Beckett's 1989 Color Dreams game, *Crystal Mines*, you control a cute little WALL*E-like robot as he digs deep beneath a planet for crystals, avoiding and sometimes murdering the "alien" natives who get in his way. It is foretold that if you can collect and kill your way through 100 levels, you'll hit "the elusive mother lode of crystals which will make you a multi-quadrillionaire."

In each level, you move your robot through a claustrophobic two-screen enclosure, shooting "energy blasts" through dirt and enemies, bombing rocks, and collecting the crystals that will make your exit appear. One of many weird game tropes that have been normalized by time and repetition: Only once you've made enough money are you allowed to leave your enclosure for the next, so that what looked at first like capitalism reveals itself to be paying your own ransom, again and again. Or maybe the exit has been there all along, but the game understands that you're too driven to even consider leaving until all the crystals have been mined.

As you progress through the mines, your enemies get harder and you've got to be more strategic, squashing them with boulders and using temporary invincibility to ghost past them to the treasures they guard. Repeating monotonously throughout is an intense little music track that sounds like a discarded theme from the Game Boy version of *Tetris*.

In many parts of the internet, *Crystal Mines* is offered the damning honor of "the Color Dreams game that's actually fun." Even Dan Lawton, Color Dreams's founder and toughest critic, acknowledges a grudging respect for the game: "*Crystal Mines* was probably the best gameplay. It certainly got the best letters from buyers."

So when it was time to start making Bible games, Lawton and company got to work adapting their cave crawler for the Christian bookstore set. The only problem was: There aren't any classic Bible stories about digging through caves and searching for treasure. So the team got creative.

·

Wisdom Tree followed its hit, *Bible Adventures*, with a game called *Exodus* (1991), which pretends to tell the biblical story of Moses leading the Israelites out of Egypt and into the Promised Land.

But in the actual gameplay, the Israelites are strangely absent, and you instead guide Moses through what appears to be an underground cave. That's because

Exodus is the same game as *Crystal Mines*, reskinned and with new levels, but with identical core mechanics.

Here, the energy bursts become W's that stand for "the Word of God," which you use to "stop the murmurings of the Israelites," represented in the game by square clods of dirt, to fight "doubting God," which is like the clods of dirt but is green and takes an extra hit to destroy, and to fight "obstacles to faith," which appear to be boulders. But don't worry, you also get to use your Word of God to kill plenty of soldiers, taskmasters, magicians, and sorcerers. The crystals are now replaced with manna, but here you also must locate all five of the question mark squares, which represent the Bible questions you'll be asked between the levels.

Also blocking your path are indestructible bricks and boulders that represent both the "limitations of man" and the "weakness of man." Power-ups include the "armor of God," distinctly unsymbolic "new sandals," and "greater faith," which grants invincibility but is, like many moments of true faith, poetically fleeting. Along the way you can pick up "the staff of Moses," which explodes on a timer like a robot's bombs would.

I'm belaboring the item descriptions in this game simply to marvel at the game's metaphysical looseness, at how comfortably *Exodus* vacillates between the spiritual/metaphorical and the physical. To review: I'm guiding an actual Moses through an actual wilderness, foraging for actual manna, but to traverse the actual wilderness, I must shoot the Word of God to quiet the

Murmurings of Israel, which is both a metaphor and a real, physical block of dirt that must be shot through. And I must kill actual evil sorcerers.

But to the gamer who wisely ignores all these temporal shifts in favor of having fun, *Exodus* is simply a game where you go around collecting stuff to the tune of the popular Sunday school song, "Father Abraham," which speeds up, Mario-like, as the timer approaches zero. The only other biblical aspects of *Exodus* are the quiz questions and the little illustrated Bible scenes between levels.

•

The next *Crystal Mines* clone was the one I'd played as a kid, *Joshua & the Battle of Jericho*, which Wisdom Tree released in 1992 as a pseudo-sequel to *Exodus*.

Although *Joshua* didn't introduce many new ideas to the *Crystal Mines* formula, the presentation was an all-around improvement: The levels were better-designed, gone was the grating music, and the game now included a new four-letter level code system so you could pick up where you left off.

But once again, the gameplay in *Joshua* has nothing to do with the story of Jericho. The story from the Book of Joshua goes like this: God speaks to Joshua, telling him to march the Ark of the Covenant around the city of Jericho once a day for six days. And then on the seventh day, the Israelite priests blow their horns and the walls of Jericho come crumbling down. Yay for the good guys! Once the walls are down, the Israelites mercilessly butcher every man, woman, child, and animal in the city, sparing only the family of Rahab, a cool lady who did the Israelites a solid by helping them kill everyone she knew.

There's no wall-circling, no Rahab-sparing, no baby-butchering. You're just another robed bro wandering through mazes, shooting musical notes at Hittites and picking up gold coins. Like a lot of actual religious crusaders, your motivations are much more economic than jihadist.

•

The fact that Lawton's decision to make Bible games was based on money and not faith is more the rule than the exception in retail.

Many of the biggest sellers of Christian stuff are actually the Christian-targeted arms of their flexi-theistic parent companies. Capitol Christian Music Group (home of TobyMac, Michael W. Smith, and Amy Grant) are part of Capitol Records, Zondervan and Thomas Nelson are the Christian imprints of HarperCollins (which is itself the book arm of News Corp), and the dating site ChristianMingle is run by Spark Network, which also runs JDate for Jews and LDSMingle for Mormons.

The cynical way of putting it is that these companies are squeezing dollars out of people who think that buying Christian merch is in some way supporting Christianity itself. The generous way of putting it is that the companies are offering inspirational goods to a Christian public who demands products that "get it right."

The truth, I suspect, lies somewhere in between and depends on the integrity of both the product itself and the product's handlers. The messy thing about the collision of faith and capitalism is that an atheist game designer can turn over a finished Bible game to a Christian sales rep, who sells it to an agnostic purchaser for a Christian bookstore, where the game is shelved beside a book about how Christians must help Israel defeat Palestine to hasten the End Times, and is eventually sold by a Buddhistically-inclined teenage cashier to a non-denominational aunt who worries because her nephew's religiously apathetic parents only take him to Church on Easter and Christmas.

Expecting every link on the chain to be authentically "Christian" is like expecting every company who delivered your kale to the market to be authentically "organic." Even in high school, I understood that the powers behind the Hot Topic where I bought my Swingin' Utters album didn't have the punk cred I demanded of the band itself.

This discussion is further complicated by the fact that unlike in the Jewish faith, a person's "Christian" designation is based not on culture but on a belief in the divinity of Jesus that could reverse on a dime. "Prone to wander, Lord, I feel it / Prone to leave the God I love," wrote Robert Robinson in 1757 when he was just 22, understanding the aspect of belief that is not itself a choice. I can say for myself that when I admitted the possibility that Jesus was not God, it felt not like a decision to proclaim but like a jellyfish that had washed up on the beach. I was free to pretend the jellyfish wasn't there, of course—nobody was calling me out on it—but it was. Skepticism had been traveling to me for years and now it was here. And it could always wash away again.

But even in a simpler scenario—a fervent Christian carves her own decorative crosses from wood and sells them at local craft fairs—our believer's business is not a Christian business because (with apologies to the Supreme Court) a business is not a person. While it's fair to criticize Lawton for pretending to be a Christian company and for cramming irreligious games into Christian packaging, it's also true that there's no such thing as a Christian company. Or, for that matter, a Christian game.

•

Crystal Mines is the Rosetta Stone that allows us to make sense of the existence of *Exodus* and *Joshua*. (Or perhaps more accurately, *Crystal Mines* is the Babylonian flood myth to the Bible's own Noah's Ark myth.) Why do you feel less like Old Testament heroes battling for your lives and more like solitary men mining for treasure in elaborate caves? Because *Exodus* and *Joshua* are based on a game about a robot mining for treasure in elaborate caves. The relief of going back and playing *Crystal Mines* is the absence of labored abstract concepts—the monsters are simply monsters. The bombs are simply bombs.

Future games using the *Crystal Mines* engine were less overt rip-offs: *Bible Buffet* nested its levels within a digital board game, and *Spiritual Warfare* wisely abandoned the tiny two-screen format for an open world epic.

But there was one more true *Crystal Mines* clone.

A faithful sequel, *Crystal Mines II*, became the one and only licensed Color Dreams game when, in 1992, Color Dreams (still releasing secular titles apart from the Wisdom Tree brand) licensed the game to Atari for its handheld Game Boy competitor, the Lynx, which Dan Burke described as "orphan hardware that's in the annals of history but not a lot of people had it at the time."

"The Lynx people made it easy to license," Lawton told the Warp Zone. "They were extremely helpful, and their licensing and manufacturing weren't quite as oppressive. Plus they helped market the games for you." I've got to wonder if the Atari team was also cheering for Color Dreams, who unlike Tengen had found a way to take on Nintendo.

Somehow *Crystal Mines* refuses to die. An update, *Crystal Mines II: Buried Treasure* came out for PC in 2000, and in 2010 was ported (simply as *Crystal Mines*) to both iOS and, finally, the Nintendo DS.

That's right: A Color Dreams property was ported to a Nintendo system with Nintendo's blessing. "The classic Atari Lynx game now on Nintendo DS," says the game's description, glossing over the unlicensed NES game that started it all. And there, in the lower right-hand corner of the box art: LICENSED BY NINTENDO. Too bad Color Dreams was no longer around in 2010 to enjoy the victory.

Ultimately, it'd have been unrealistic for Nintendo to hold twenty-year grudges against competitors. Nintendo is the kind of conqueror who offers its subjects a job—just look at the hardworking hedgehog on the cover of *Mario & Sonic at the Olympics*. Why say no to a perfectly good property? There's money to be made.

DREAMS OF A PLAYABLE JESUS

JESUS CHRIST IS THE JESUS CHRIST of potential video game characters.

He starts out as a humble nobody carpenter with a ton of potential, chopping down trees for his dad's shop. Then one day he's anointed by John the Baptist, from whom he receives low-level miraculous powers. To level up his newfound skills, Jesus spends a month grinding in the wilderness, battling Satan. But when he gets back to Galilee, he finds it's been overrun with demons! He's got to exorcise his way through town, driving out the demons and healing cripples. Now it's time to build his party—in a fishing minigame, he impresses Simon so much that Simon follows him and changes his name to Peter. Jesus wins the loyalty of his twelve apostles, each of whom has a unique skill—fishing, tax collecting, doubting, betraying—and once an apostle joins his team, Jesus can select any two of the twelve to accompany him on missions. He heals lepers, replenishes health by eating with sinners, raises the dead, feeds multitudes, battling demons all the while. By the time he reaches level 10, Jesus can perform the Transfiguration, a move that summons Moses and Elijah to wipe all enemies from the vicinity. Eventually Jesus collects enough gold to purchase a donkey, which he rides into the city of Jerusalem. He is arrested, tried, and killed for the sins of humanity via quick cutscene and then does battle with Satan once again—this time banishing Satan for good.

The story of Jesus, as I just told it, could be an RPG, a Metroidvania platformer, or, best of all, a 3D semi-open world action-adventure game. If you've played Wisdom Tree's 1991 three-in-one Jesus game, *King of Kings: The Early Years*, you already know it is none of these things.

This was not accidental. "We stayed away from anything that could be considered blasphemy," Dan Lawton said. "The idea we came up with was, no one should play God. […] God is out. Jesus is out. Everyone else is okay."

Mostly, *King of Kings* is a game about animals. In "The Wise Men," you're a camel carrying a Wise Man to the birth of Jesus, but lizards and cacti keep attacking you and you have to spit on them. In "Flight to Egypt," you're a donkey carting Joseph, Mary, and Baby Jesus to Egypt, but snakes and mountain goats keep attacking you so you have to kill them with your ineffectual donkey kick. The mission ends when you leap over a polar bear.

Lawton wondered if even spitting camels could be too controversial for a sensitive Christian audience. "I remember when we were working on *King of Kings*," Huff told me. "Dan Lawton was worried that parents would think we were teaching their kids to spit. We had three meetings on this subject. I thought this was ludicrous. Finally, I blurted out, 'God made camels and camels spit!' They never let me forget that comment."

But then, in a *Bible Adventures* retread called "Jesus and the Temple," you're Joseph, solo this time, racing back to the temple upon realizing that you *Home Alone*'d the Son of God. Like Kevin McCallister, Jesus is fending for himself just fine, teaching some adults a thing or two in the process, and will have a few precocious words for Joseph upon his breathless return. "Why were you searching for me?" Jesus will ask his adopted dad. "Didn't you know I had to be in my Father's house?"

But you, as Joseph, don't know that yet, so you must race back to Jesus while avoiding bees that want to kill you. In yet another *Super Mario Bros. 2* reference, little logs float conveniently down waterfalls so that you may skip across them to safety.

King of Kings had all the makings of a cash grab sequel—rehashed *Bible Adventures* mechanics, diminishing returns, and less-plausible premises. If I asked you to come up with a dozen ideas for Bible games, "Joseph racing against time to find Jesus, who has been hanging out dropping wisdom in the temple, but Joseph doesn't know that," would probably not have been on your list. It's a scenario fraught only with parental misunderstanding.

In yet another parallel, games in both *Bible Adventures* and *King of Kings* find their stakes in parents' desire to protect their kids. A video game about a parent working hard to protect their child is pretty humane, and more relatable than your standard kidnapping plot. Even if one of those playable parents is about to send her kid downriver in a basket.

•

The other night I had pho with a friend who has been putting all the pieces together to create his own indie game development company. I asked him how his robot game was going, and he told me that the robot game was so ambitious that they now planned to release a couple of simpler games beforehand.

First up: *SCIENCE CANNON!* A tower defense game where you're working to build a supercannon so you can "shoot science at God." You choose from one of twelve historical scientists, each with his or her own special ability—Tesla, for instance, zaps enemies with his Tesla Coil. The enemies? Priests, clergy, monks, Scientologists, Mormons on bicycles…

"What about Mohammed?" I said. "Are you gonna depict him?"

"We had a discussion about that. Yes. You'll blow him up along with Jesus and everyone else."

I said, "I hope no one kills you!"

"I know it'll offend some people, but it's all very campy," he said. "I mean, the title's in all caps and there's an exclamation point at the end. Are you offended?"

"No," I said, and repeated, "I just really hope no one kills you." And then added, "But if no one kills you it sounds like a cool game."

•

Religion has an uneasy relationship with depiction.

The word iconoclast, from the Greek *eikon* (image) and *klastes* (breaker), has its roots in literal image-breaking. The Byzantine (eastern Roman) emperor Leo III led a government-sponsored iconoclastic campaign sometime around 730, destroying Christian icons as idols.

The problem is that the difference between an icon and an idol is one of perception: An icon is used as an aid through which to worship God... unless you begin to worship the icon itself, at which point it becomes an idol. So if, while in prayer, you kiss your Mary figurine too feverishly, I can think of at least two reasons you might make your priest uncomfortable.

Today, a church's approach to iconography depends on what flavor the church is: Catholic churches will hang a lifelike, suffering Christ on their walls while most Protestant churches prefer a bare, simple cross, but both Catholics and Protestants have no problem depicting Jesus in art, so long as it's respectful.

So why no *real* Jesus games from Wisdom Tree or anyone else?[9]

Because a video game is like an icon—whether or not it is a "respectful" game depends entirely on how you play it. And since our hypothetical Jesus game would be no fun at all if it didn't take Jesus's godhood as a given (I demand *powers*), the game would immediately encounter ludonarrative dissonance. A term coined by Clint Hocking to help explain the shortcomings of the original *BioShock*, ludonarrative dissonance refers to instances in a video game where there's a clear conflict between a game's story and its gameplay.

What if, in our open-world game, Jesus refuses to use his healing powers on lepers, skipping their colony entirely? What if Jesus starts following a prostitute around long after he's forgiven her sins? What if Jesus takes an axe made to cut trees and turns it on the children of Galilee? In what might be the most egregious instances of ludonarrative dissonance ever performed in a game, the Son of God would start to look a lot less perfect.

Or even if you don't choose to play like a jerk, what if you simply play *poorly*? If you die early in a game of *Jesus Adventures*, is that a rectifiable bummer in the video game tradition of "if at first you don't succeed," or

---

9   I'm choosing not to count the jokey fun of M. Dickie's *The You Testament*, though you should absolutely check it out.

is your death the too-early fulfillment of God's will for all of humankind?

While an open-world Jesus game would certainly be used for mischief, I wonder whether it might attract just as many gamers who'd rather play as Jesus the paragon than as Jesus the renegade. Could the game be played with kindness? Even conviction?

Ian Bogost's *How to Do Things with Videogames* is a book of short essays in which the author, under the premise that "understanding games as a medium of leisure or productivity alone is insufficient," dedicates each chapter-essay to a thing games have accomplished before and could do again: Art, Empathy, Kitsch, Titillation, Exercise, and even things we might wish games wouldn't do, like Promotion. "Videogames are often accused of disrespect, especially for celebrating violence and encouraging disdain of man, woman, and culture alike," Bogost says in his chapter on Reverence. "But can a game do the opposite, embracing respect, deference, even reverence?"

Interestingly, he mentions not a single overtly religious game in this chapter. This is no accidental oversight. "Wisdom Tree's games did not proceduralize religious faith," Bogost writes in another book, *Persuasive Games*. "Instead, they borrowed the operational logics of platform and adventure games, applying vaguely religious or biblical situations atop the familiar gestures of moving, shooting, and jumping."

Instead of discussing *Bible Adventures* or its contemporaries, Bogost summarizes the controversy over *Resistance: Fall of Man*'s recreation of the Manchester Cathedral, which in the game has been wrecked by alien invaders by the time your hero happens upon it. The Church of England was outraged that the makers of *Resistance* would use one of their actual cathedrals instead of making one up, but to Bogost the Church missed the point: It'd be one thing if your character fired a rocket launcher at the cathedral out of a nihilistic *Grand Theft Auto*-like sense of "why the hell not," but the game treats the cathedral's devastation as a real loss for humanity—as if the aliens have desecrated something truly holy.

When cognitive anthropologist Ryan Horbeck studied Chinese *World of Warcraft* players, he found that *WoW* players often reported feelings of spiritual transcendence. One player called the game "an unconditional feast of spiritual loyalty and friendship."

PBS Game/Show's Jamin Warren credits this, in part, to the natural buy-in that comes with playing any sort of game—we submit ourselves to the game's laws, retreating for a time from the real world—so transcendence is the next step in the natural immersion of gaming. He goes on to point out that Blizzard built strong social ties right into *WoW*, and that community is integral to spiritual experience. If you've ever felt the universe briefly click into place while singing at the top of your lungs alongside hundreds of other people, you understand.

To other critics, the spiritual gains to be found in games are minimal. "There are, of course, many ways in which religious stories, characters, and themes can be and are integrated into video games," writes Robert M. Geraci in his article "Video Games and the Transhuman Inclination," "but these provide only minimal access to transcendent experiences or states of being, even when the games are specifically religious."

Part of what I think we're seeing in this conversation is a struggle to find common ground among individuals with radically different belief systems. Is it possible to have a spiritual experience if God doesn't show up? Is it possible to revere a God you don't totally believe in?

I'm on the fence. It's clearly possible for a game to enable what feels like a spiritually transcendent experience, but that could only happen if the game was being put to the service of the spiritual experience. In *WoW*, unity, teamwork, and virtue are built into the DNA of the game—the euphoria one feels while playing it is *designed*, even if the game's designers did not themselves frame it in spiritual terms. In Bogost's example of *Resistance*, the cathedral is deployed for pathos, but only as a means to an end. The sense of loss drives the player's desire to get payback on the alien shitbags who desecrated our monument, our icon—not to offer a testament to the power of God.

Not that I see this as a problem. One of the weirder conventions of so many religions and particularly Christianity, Judaism, and Islam is the portrayal of God as a big baby who is never more upset than when someone portrays him in anything but the kindest light. "It's in the Ten Commandments to not take the Lord's name in vain," goes a Louis C.K. bit. "Rape is not up there, by the way. Rape is not a Ten Commandment. But don't say the dude's name with a shitty attitude." My own suspicion is that if there's a God, he/she/it/they can probably stomach a little more sacrilege than we've been trained to think.

Which leads me back to Jesus, a guy much more concerned with being the right person than with practicing the right rituals.

Surely we can handle depicting Jesus as a playable character. We could kill afternoons in the sandals of history's best-loved and most deeply misrepresented peacemaker. We could post our favorite moments of ludonarrative dissonance to YouTube. Maybe we could even get a little training-wheels practice at being in the presence of the destitute people who so many of our mass-market games turn into a punchline, *help* those people instead of stabbing them, and remember in the process that they are, in fact, people, and thus worthy of love and compassion and food.

If the Catholic Church gets to present their blood-sweating Lord upon every wall and column, if Mel Gibson gets to make Christ play out his every BDSM fantasy on screen for sold-out theaters across the world, surely a game company will have the balls to put the player in control of Jesus and then let that player decide what kind of Jesus she wants to be.

THROW A BIBLE IN IT

IN 1990, NOT LONG BEFORE they began making Wisdom Tree titles, Color Dreams came out with a truly worldly game that, had it been licensed by Nintendo, would have never made it past Nintendo's censors.

Menace Beach stars Scooter, a young skateboard punk—blond in the box art, black-haired in the game—whose sassy girlfriend, Bunny, has been kidnapped by Demon Dan, a villain Nina Stanley created to look like her boss, Dan Lawton.

This was just one of the game's several inside jokes. Scooter was based on Nina Stanley's seven-year-old son, a surfer enemy was based on her coworker Jim Treadway, and then there was Suki Yashi, a sumo wrestler who appears to be based on American WWII propaganda aimed specifically at dehumanizing the Japanese. But in fact, Suki was based on Color Dreams's lead game testers, a pair of obese high school dropouts that the development team called the "Sumo Brothers."

A frantic sidescroller with abysmal hit detection, *Menace Beach* is another game in which avoiding objects as they're hurled at you is a full-time job. Scooter scoots through beaches and sewers to rescue his love, who in a common video game trope, communicates directly to Scooter through girlfriend ESP between levels: "Listen up, Dog Breath!" begins one message. "If you're still planning on that date at the malt shop, you'd better get me out of this mess now, nerd."

But more important than Bunny's taunts is that her clothes fall off a little more between each level. Seeing just how much comes off is intended to be the player's chief motivation for pressing on. Time or Demon Dan eventually strips Bunny down to her bra and panties before the last level, but instead of the fully nude humpfest ending the thirteen-year-old male demographic is teased with, the credits end with Scooter and a fully-clothed Bunny on a wholesome malt shop date, gazing chastely into one another's eyes.

There *is*, however, an actual pornographic version of *Menace Beach*. *Miss Peach World* (1991), released only in Asian territories by a company called Hacker International, subs out Scooter for a white-haired Marilyn Monroe clone and shows pixelated drawings of naked women in between levels. The Peach referenced in the title is Princess Toadstool herself, the cover art portraying a big-breasted Peach floating happily away from an angry Cheep Cheep fish, but Peach (and, for that matter, Cheep Cheep) appear nowhere in the game.

•

To their credit, the Color Dreams team had nothing to do with the *Miss Peach World* hack. It would take them several more years before they would bastardize *Menace Beach* themselves.

In fact, they waited so long to do it that the resulting Wisdom Tree title, *Sunday Funday: The Ride*, would bear the dubious honor of becoming The Last NES Game Ever Produced. 1995, the year *Sunday Funday* was released to an unnoticing public, also saw the release of *Mortal Kombat 3*, *Tekken 2*, *Twisted Metal*, and *Warcraft II: Tides of Darkness*. The world was nearly nostalgic for old NES titles, not hungry for new ones. (To be fair, Wisdom Tree was also porting four of their NES games to Sega Genesis in a bid for continued relevance, but they updated the games' graphics only marginally.)

So what is *Sunday Funday*, the historic Last Game, like? In short: It's a hell of lot like *Menace Beach*.

Each of the games in the Wisdom Tree catalogue could be pretty easily divided into two categories. (1) Games that were clearly conceived of as "Christian": *Bible Adventures*, *King of Kings*, *Spiritual Warfare*. The makers of these games, while mostly not Christians themselves, are clearly asking themselves, "What would Christians want?" and delivering on that as best they can. (2) Pre-existing Color Dreams games modded to look Christian: *Exodus*, *Joshua*, *Bible Buffet*, and *Sunday Funday*. In honor of *Sunday Funday*, I propose we call them "Throw a Bible in It" games, or TABII for short.

The protagonist of *Sunday Funday* is an unnamed young man who looks exactly like Scooter from *Menace Beach*, but with one important difference: a Bible has been digitally inserted into his hands.

His mission has changed as well. No longer is Scooter trying to rescue a girlfriend with a taste for easily dissolved clothes, he's just a sweet kid trying to get to church on time. If only the jerks in his town would let him! It seems this is the Sunday everyone is against you: Sailor Sammy, Businessman Bert, Plumber Pete. "Who are these raging atheists that don't want you to go to church?" asks the Angry Video Game Nerd (AVGN) in his YouTube video on the game. And while the manual has it that each member of the heathen townsfolk simply wants your assistance unplugging drains, scraping barnacles, and mowing lawns—"None of the things they have to offer should stop you," warns the game's manual—the in-game mechanics make it clear that they're actually out for blood.

And so, apparently, are you. While some of your unholy distractors can simply be ignored, the sidescroll often halts, *Double Dragon*-like, until your enemy has been properly disposed of. In *Double Dragon*, this made a certain sense—these thugs are from the gang who stole your girl! (Probably!) Here, the mechanic makes it clear that your job is not merely to make it alive to Sunday school, but to have murdered as many townsfolk along the way as possible. For all you squeamish peacemakers, the game's manual reminds us to "remember what is most important; going to Sunday school to learn from the Bible."

For *Sunday Funday*, Demon Dan wouldn't do as a final boss—demons are nothing to joke about—so Dan is replaced with Big Brown Bear. And why not? It worked fine for the end of the donkey game in *King of Kings*. Here, the manual does not attempt to build up the bear with any epic lore, or even a single attribute, but says simply, "Hey! where did this guy come from! No need to worry, you can get past this because we know that 'all things are possible with God.'"

In place of Malt Shop Bunny is your Sunday school teacher, whose red dress and matching heels unfortunately stay on for the entirety of the game, but she does encourage you in your violent journey and warn you about the dangers you'll soon face: "If you pass the plumber, he will try to slow you down!"

Interestingly, though, each of her encouragements is prefaced with the explanation, "You imagine what your Sunday school teacher would say." This clarifies how she's communicating with you and nicely circumvents the potentially occult practice of ESP. However, the prescience of her advice—sure enough, there's a plumber to avoid—hints that our hero may not be going through this ordeal for the first time. Maybe this Sunday slaughterfest is a weekly thing. *How many must die for this sociopath to get to church on time?*

•

Even though *Sunday Funday* is the inspiration for the term TABII, which I'll redefine as "any product that appears to have been hastily rebranded for Christian consumption," it's not the only TABII offered by Wisdom Tree. It's not even the only TABII offered in the *Sunday Funday* cart.

Billed as another three-in-one, *Sunday Funday* contains a puzzler called "Fish Fall" where you catch falling fish and toss them up into a basket. If this doesn't sound particularly biblical, it's because it's entirely based on a game Roger Deforest programmed in his spare time from his bedroom in Newport Beach. Its working title was "Hand Job," but in its completed form was called "Free Fall."

Originally inspired by *Lemmings*, Deforest conceived of a game where "instead of the little people falling down and dying, you had to catch them and throw them into a basket to save them," so he simply started creating it. Deforest enjoyed having full creative control for once. "I could build any level and any type of enemy I wanted to without having to answer to Lawton, Eddy, or the Sumos. Since I had the skills to do the coding, artwork, and music, nothing stopped me from just making a game that I wanted to play."

The game Deforest wanted to play had the visual palette and all the eccentricity of an Adult Swim show: A giant hand caught little guys called the Quirks before they could fall to their deaths and tossed them up into a Mario-like green pipe. It's later revealed that the suicidal Quirks are under the mind control of a blue-faced boss named Squishi who is thankfully vulnerable to pickles. Upon Squishi's defeat, six Quirks hoist the giant hand above their heads for a parade through the city. Here's Deforest, explaining everything about this premise: "I was heavily into the Dada movement."

Deforest hadn't expected to sell the game to his own employer, much less for it to be adapted into a Wisdom Tree title, but Lawton was impressed with "Free Fall" and approached him to buy it. Vance Kozik, in charge of the negotiation, offered Deforest $1,200 for the game. Deforest scoffed and asked for $7,000. Kozik laughed at the number, but Lawton agreed to it. Deforest signed over the exclusive rights to "Free Fall," and Nina Stanley set out to Christianize it.

This time, the TABII element was not a Bible, but another symbol close to the heart of Christianity: the fish. The *ichthys*—the elegantly simple fish symbol you'll recognize from the bumper stickers of SUVs that cut you off on the freeway—was used by the early Christians as a secret handshake while under the very real danger of the Roman Empire.

The fish in the Stanley's Christianized version, now called "Fish Fall," was not an ichthys but a real oceanic fish. Before the first level, we get a Bible verse, "Follow me and I will make you fishers of men" (Matthew 4:18), and then we're off and running, tossing fish (instead of people) into baskets.

Thankfully, "Fish Fall" is no less weird than "Free Fall." And when fish parachute down into your waiting hand, get shot out of a cannon, or hoist the giant hand up for a parade in their undersea kingdom, it might actually be even weirder. Ultimately, the only connection between the game and Christendom is that fish are one of the more prominent nouns that appear in the Bible.

An unexpected thing happened as I played "Fish Fall"—I realized I was *having fun*. Not "*GoldenEye* with three friends" fun, but I was pretty into it, and I wondered why this little throwaway tacked-on game was enjoyable in a way that the main event was not.

The reason I've arrived at? It's a game of skill. Timing is everything. You have to determine when to focus on catching fish, when to focus on throwing, and when you can both throw and catch in the same motion. In later levels, there are hoppy creatures to avoid. The challenge escalates moderately, a sense of flow is achieved, and the more you play, the better you get. If you don't have your wits about you, you will not pass to the next stage. "Fish Fall" exists firmly within the *Tetris/Dr. Mario/Breakout/Bust-a-Move* puzzler genre without too blatantly ripping off any one of them. I don't want to make too much of "Fish Fall"—it's too slight to join the pantheon of great puzzlers—but what separates "Fish Fall" from most of the other Wisdom Tree games is that it is so clearly a game.[10]

---

10   What *isn't* clearly a game is the third selection rounding out *Sunday Funday*'s advertised three-in-one bundle, which is nothing but an 8-bit rendition of "The Ride," a song by the marginally popular Christian pop group 4Him. The lyrics appear onscreen so you can karaoke along. That's it—that's the whole "game."

When I asked him what he thought of the Christian version, Deforest said, "I thought it was cute, but it lost the edginess and non sequitur I was going for. To this day I'd rather play 'Free Fall.'" Several years ago, Deforest released the code for the original version so fans could do just that. Now ROMs of both "Fish Fall" and "Free Fall" are available online, and anyone with an emulator can decide once and for all whether they want to be Christian catchers of fish or secular fishers of men.

•

Wisdom Tree's most egregious TABII game is the one in which the Bible never appears beyond the title screen.

Conceived of as a combination "family board game" (think *Candy Land*) and yet another *Crystal Mines* level crawler, *Bible Buffet* (1993) is the limpest turd of a game. You wander through a colorful world where both the prizes and the enemies are food. What the levels present is a less a challenge and more a colorful couple of frames to wander through as you make your way up to the exit. You can kill baddies and collect food if you want, or not. It's entirely up to you.

Certain enemies are impenetrable, but you can run past them, lose a bit of life, and probably come out fine. When you die, it's consequence-free. The game advises you try again, and you start over with full life. If you die three times on the same stage, the game simply moves on as if you've completed it.

The board game scenario nicely ensures that you won't have to play through every level, but in the design of nearly every level, it seems as if the game's creators reasoned, "Well, players won't usually land on *this* stage," and gave themselves a pass to make it barely functional.

The few power-ups don't matter, so your main incentive is to blitz past the levels—they offer nothing and do not grow in complexity or, with a couple of weirdly hard exceptions, difficulty. But "hard" never means "challenging" in *Bible Buffet*. You will not be rewarded for time spent perfecting technique. You will only be sad that you lingered in a game that offers so few pleasures. When you beat the game, it tells you who was first to finish and who ate the most food, then it goes straight back to the start screen.

The titular buffet is clear—food is absolutely everywhere. But where's the Bible?

Only in the trivia.

•

Even at my most devout, Bible trivia was never my strong suit.

When I was growing up and going to Bible class on Sunday and Wednesday nights, we often played a trivia game called Bible Bowl. It was during Bible Bowl that I learned that several of my friends' families took the study of the Bible extremely seriously, much more so than my parents did. I'd absorbed enough that I might be able to answer a question where the answer is Zacchaeus, ark, or Ten Commandments, but not any of the questions where the answer is Boaz, 300 cubits long, or the tribe of Benjamin.

Once a year, my church took our collective Bible skills on the road. They'd charter a bus to take the kids and teens to the Opryland Hotel in Nashville, TN, so that we could compete against the kids from other Churches of Christ throughout the South in such categories as Preaching, Song-Leading, Scripture-Reading, Bible Bowl, and my favorite, Puppet Show. It was in puppet rehearsals that I learned the rules of puppetry, the hardest of which was also the most important: Even though your wrist is incredibly tired, do not point your hand up in the air or your puppet will look straight up at the sky.

The competition was called Lads to Leaders/Leaderettes. The diminutive made-up word "leaderettes" was a pretty good indicator of the old school conservatism at the heart of the conference. Women were allowed their own preaching competition, but no men (not even the girl's own father) could be in the room because women preaching to men was *not okay*. My own progressive consciousness wouldn't wake up for a decade, so none of this bugged me. Mostly I remember the jungle theme of the Opryland lobby, the fun of being on a trip away from parents, of staying up late with friends, of the possibility (though not the occurrence) of meeting girls. I competed in several events, but never Bible Bowl. It seemed the preacher's son just didn't have the chops for it.

Wisdom Tree craftily built a learning component into each of their games to appeal to kids like me. *Little Gabe not reading his Bible enough? There's Bible verses and/or trivia in every game!*

How you get to the trivia changes from game to game. In *Bible Adventures*, you simply read verses off tablets and get an extra unit of health, even if you skip quickly past it, and verses in *Sunday Funday* are similarly skippable. In *King of Kings*, though, you instead collect scrolls and must answer a question correctly to get the extra health. In *Joshua* and *Exodus*, sets of questions show up between levels. In *Bible Buffet*, you're asked to refer to a quiz book that comes with the game and are presented only with a question number and the letters A, B, C, and D.[11] And in *Spiritual Warfare*, if you convert/kill enough guys, an angel floats aimlessly onscreen in the manner of the *Zelda* fairy upon which the angel was clearly based. Catch the staggering angel and he quizzes you.

If Noah or David or Moses's mom or Moses himself or Joseph or the camel or the donkey or Joshua or the

---

11   Asking players to venture out-game is the worst, and has thankfully fallen out of vogue. The end of this trend may have something to do with the mass confusion caused by the NES game *StarTropics* (1990), which required you to dip a real-world note into water for a secret password.

Sunday School Attendee Formerly Known as Scooter or the Lord's Warrior answers his or her questions correctly, you are ever rewarded with the same, most precious thing: health itself, the promise or possibility that you shall not perish but have everlasting life. Unless you get shot, stabbed, mauled, drowned, or blown up.

Luckily, the questions in the Wisdom Tree games tilt toward the easy, and are rife with context clues. "God desires that _____ be saved and come to know the knowledge of the truth," goes one wordy fill-in-the-blank question. Your available answers are "no one," "all men," and "good people." Many of the true/false questions are likewise gimmes: "True or False: Jesus never quoted scripture." And "True or False: Jesus said it is okay to commit adultery."

Other times, though, you picture the quizmaster opening a Bible and writing a question based on the very specific wording of a particular passage. "John the Baptist preached for men to repent and _____ the gospel." The options are "listen to," "read," and "believe." They want you to pick "believe," but you can't believe without either listening or reading.

The most truly biblical Wisdom Tree titles were a pair of "games" for the Game Boy: *King James Bible* and *NIV Bible & the 20 Lost Levels of Joshua*. The games are what they sound like—two different translations of the Bible. "Step aside, *Super Mario Land*," wrote the Religious News Service upon the games' release, and the back cover of *King James* advised, "Keep a fresh set of batteries around—you'll be reading this Bible a lot," but the cartridges didn't approach the success of Wisdom Tree's most popular games. Can you imagine reading any book on the yellow-green screen of the original Game Boy? Let alone a book that's 774,746 words long?

A quick googling reports that Lads to Leaders/Leaderettes is going strong in 2015, with annual conferences in Atlanta, Dallas, Louisville, Memphis, and Orlando. Minister William Hardy Jr. raves of the event, "If we would have had this program, the young men I grew up with would not be in jail and dead today." Their site also brags that while only half of Church of Christ members stick with their denomination after high school, "many congregations with Lads to Leaders/Leaderettes have a 92-100% youth retention rate!" I guess you can't argue with hard data.

I never did become a Bible trivia master, but I do understand a lot more of the psychology of test-writing than I used to, which means that when I play Wisdom Tree games now as an adult, I dominate most of the quiz questions.

For instance: If a true/false question says that according to Luke 8:12, Chad 3:16, Hebrews 6:4,000, or any verse at all, "Jesus was an awesome guy," mark it True. Technically they are quizzing you about your knowledge of that particular verse, but if the answer was False, it would look as if Wisdom Tree was saying, "Jesus was not an awesome guy." And we simply can't have that.

SPIRITUAL WARRIORS

THE LITERALIZATION OF SPIRITUAL WARFARE is one of the stickiest, war-hawkiest, and most blockbuster concepts to ever come out of the New Testament.

As Christianity's more excitable denominations would have it: Every day, actual angels and demons duke it out on a celestial CGI battlefield over your littlest temptations. Snuck a twenty-spot out of Mom's wallet? Some sporty demon landed a sucker punch. Resisted the call of the PornHub for the entirety of Memorial Day weekend? Must've been a big win for the good guys. A fringe benefit to this way of viewing the universe is that it takes the moral imperative off a body's own free will: It's not your fault when you're bad. The corpses stacked in your meat locker merely imply that Satan's really been on his game lately.

"Therefore put on the full armor of God," says Paul in his Letter to the Ephesians, "so that when the day of evil comes, you may be able to stand your ground. [...] Stand firm then, with the belt of truth buckled around your waist, with the breastplate of righteousness in place, and with your feet fitted with the readiness that comes from the gospel of peace. In addition to all this, take up the shield of faith, with which you can extinguish all the flaming arrows of the evil one. Take the helmet of salvation and the sword of the Spirit, which is the word of God."

A zealously violent Jew who used to slaughter Christians just because he thought they were wrong about who God is, Paul naturally trafficked in battle metaphors even when all he had to say was: Have faith, be righteous, and—*ha*—be peaceful.

Wisdom Tree's 1992 game *Spiritual Warfare* elegantly combines the heavens and the earth by putting you in control of a little guy in a big world much like our own—dirty, dangerous, bound for ruin—but whose connection to the spiritual world is more concrete. Angels arrive early and often to command you, to chastise you, and to power you up with newer better weapons so that you can do the Lord's work—kickin' ass.

Well. *Sort of* kickin' ass.

Though it's easy to forget it for the game's 8-bit ambiguities, your main weapons are thrown fruits, and not just any fruits but the Fruits of the Spirit, which Paul, this time in his Letter to the Galatians, tells us are "love, joy, peace, patience, kindness, goodness, faithfulness, gentleness, and self-control." But since you can't throw a gentleness at an unbeliever, these Fruits, like the Armor of God, are literalized into pears, apples, and grapes.

If *Super Mario Bros. 2*'s "pick things up and throw them" gameplay offered the basic template for *Bible Adventures*, the game that most clearly inspired *Warfare* is *The Legend of Zelda*. You've got the big overworld, ripe for exploration but closed off in certain areas until you've powered up, and the mazelike interiors, some of which run deep and contain bosses. You move frame by frame, and the enemies repopulate if you get far enough away from them. You start small and weak, but are gifted your primary weapon in the very first room (up and to the left) and grow from there. Your mission is that of the collector/assembler, who must in this case obtain every piece of the Armor of God to fight Satan. Your keys, torches, rafts, and potions all do what you'd think. Your bombs (here called "Vials of the Wrath of God") bust through walls and unbelievers alike. You've got stores peddling wares, some of which are essential. You've even got select little rooms that operate with a newfound platformer-like respect for gravity (a la *Zelda*'s dungeon ladder power-up rooms) before abandoning it once again.

Another thing *Warfare* shares with *Zelda*: It's a lot of fun. Probably the most fun game in the Color Dreams/ Wisdom Tree catalogue. A mystery of the NES age is that for how enjoyable and lucrative *The Legend of Zelda* was, imitators did not come out of the woodwork the way *Mario* clones did. It's possible that a *Zelda* clone, with its vast sprawling maps, would take longer to code than your average run-n-jump platformer, but sprawling maps didn't stop Enix from churning out a *Dragon Quest* annually for three years straight. When *Zelda*'s much-anticipated sequel arrived, *The Adventure of Link* failed to satisfy our craving as it was mostly a platformer. The greatest *Zelda*-inspired game for the NES console, SNK's *Crystalis*, arrived too late for the world to take notice. *Warfare*, with its own big explorable world, scratched a powerful itch for kids who, like me, belonged to both the Christian bookstore and *Nintendo Power* set.

The map of *Warfare* is not a fantasy world of caves, dragons, and tunics, but a contemporary one of cars, trains, construction workers, and high-rise buildings—it's just that there are demons and advice-offering angels behind every corner, and the Truth is known only by a privileged few. These few are tasked with venturing out into a fallen world, spreading the Truth, and (if necessary) killing those without ears to listen. It is, in other words, the real world as seen through the eyes of a fundamentalist.

•

Twice in high school, I went to a weeklong evangelism training conference in Costa Mesa, CA called Students Equipped to Minister to Peers (SEMP). If Lads to Leaders/Leaderettes was training in how to be a good Christian boy on Sunday mornings, SEMP was training in how to take those skills to the streets. And while its face was a lot more casual, SEMP's roots were more deeply conservative than Lads to Leaders or any other institution I'd encountered before.

At many times of day, SEMP was just like the church camps and retreats I was attending at that time: We slept in college dorms, went to classes, listened to sermons, and sang for an hour each night.

It was the afternoons that made SEMP unique. Every day after lunch, we'd divide up into teams and then head out in vans to a nearby beach where we would evangelize to unsuspecting sunbathers. Equipped with evangelical tracts, carefully honed personal testimonies, and recently-learned stats proving the Bible's veracity,[12] we went umbrella to umbrella, towel to towel, in search of prospective converts.

I tried to be a good sport, a good spiritual warrior, but those afternoon outings were my personal Hell. I've always hated bugging people, so when out on those beach missions, I secretly hoped most interactions would be speedy and innocuous. Often when my SEMP team ran into another SEMP team on the beach, we'd

---

12   For instance, we were told that there were 300+ prophecies of the coming of Jesus in the Old Testament. According to the SEMP manual, the odds of this occurring coincidentally "would be as likely as filling up the state of Texas two feet deep with silver dollars and marking one coin, stirring the whole mass of coins thoroughly and blindfolding a man and telling him he can travel as far as he wishes, but he must pick up one silver dollar and say that this is the one."

all linger and chat awhile, eager for a distraction from our Great Commission.

When I invited a beachgoer to chat, the only thing worse than her responding with a clipped "no thanks" was her saying sure: She'd be glad to hear the story of a personal experience with Jesus Christ from a gawky teen trying not to stare at her nearly bare tits. The ultimate goal was to guide the sunbather through a prayer in which she accepts Christ into her heart, to give her info on a local church she could plug into, and to send her back out into the world a changed woman. As in *Spiritual Warfare*, she would at this point no longer be my concern—after being converted, she'd drop to her knees, say her prayer, and disappear.

One day, I met a middle-aged Taoist guy who told me (with what even then felt like scary prescience) that I was young and that my views would someday evolve. Another day, I met a kind and chatty lesbian and talked to her awhile, only to find out the next day that if you encounter One of the Gays, you are to abort mission immediately.

Going home in the van each evening, I was sick with guilt. Day after day, my personal conversion count remained zero. Meanwhile my friend Aaron absolutely crushed it. Not only did he pray the prayer with a bunch of people, he took a couple of those converts out into the ocean and baptized them on the spot. I knew it wasn't just luck—I'd never be an Aaron. Each morning in training our leader would say, "Hands up: How many of you saved someone yesterday?" We'd tally our conversion numbers for the week, lower per capita for deadweights like me.

Still, I sang hard at night and had serious, important faith talks with my best friend, Brent. A few days into the conference, Brent's first-ever girlfriend broke up with him, and in his grief Brent immediately skimmed through a popular Christian abstinence tome called *I Kissed Dating Goodbye*. He had me sign a sheet as a witness to his new commitment to never kiss another girl until it was at the altar, a commitment he kept for nearly three weeks. The next year, Brent confessed to me in confidence that he'd begun to doubt God's existence altogether, and instead of keeping that confidence I immediately gathered a group of our friends to emergency-pray for his soul.

Fervor was the style at the time. Those weeks at SEMP, we flirted with an intense fundamentalism that was impossible to maintain in our normal lives. We were taught to believe that faith was the highest stakes game there was. That it was literally, as SEMP's promotional video twice states, "a matter of life and death."

•

When in *Spiritual Warfare* you kill heathens (or "Unsaved Souls" as the manual calls them), it's understood that your well-placed apple to the head has not murdered the heathen, it has set him free. The heathen suddenly drops to his knees, mouths a brief prayer, and disappears forever.

Our hero's fruit-barrage technique works wonders when it comes to bringing dangerous heathens to their knees. But about one out of five times, that's not all it does: Even before the mortal has disappeared from the map, the demon inside is unleashed and attacks you. He must be felled in the same manner as his vessel: more fruit.

This convention was eventually skewered in an episode of *The Simpsons*. While in the home of mega-Christians Rod and Todd Flanders, Bart fires up their game, *Billy Graham's Bible Blaster*, a first-person shooter where you use a handgun to shoot Bibles at heathens, which instantly converts them to Christianity. "Got him!" Bart says after hitting an unbeliever. "No," Rod says, "you just winged him and made him a Unitarian!"

In this way, *Warfare* shares a bit of DNA with a better game, *EarthBound*, in which the New Age Retro Hippie and Annoying Old Party Man are not killed by your attacks, they're un-brainwashed: set free.

After you, as our spiritual warrior, kill/save two bikers who appear to have been terrorizing an old woman, she cryptically quotes Paul's Letter to the Romans: "But if we hope for what we do not have, we wait for it patiently." In another *EarthBound* parallel, you are to wait around in the frame for a little while. Eventually one of the cars rolls forward, revealing the stairs to a room where you may purchase a banana. (Much of your map-wandering amounts to gathering new fruits, hearts, and items to give you strength for a final confrontation.) When you're ready, you'll sneak into prison, avoiding all the perpetually rioting prisoners as best you can, and take a staircase down into Hell.

While Hell is the most moody and goth-looking part of the game, the music does not change at all. You are treated to the same singsong rendition of "On Christ the Solid Rock I Stand" that you've been hearing on repeat the whole game.

Hell is not called Hell in *Spiritual Warfare*, it's called Demon's Lair, though the pools of lava, hordes of demons, and spooky pointy hoofprints make it clear that you've come to kill Satan on his home turf. Only they don't call him Satan, either, but simply Final Boss and then "the final foe."

Why did the Wisdom Tree pull these punches? Why not call a Satan a Satan?

For one thing, it's often pretty hard to tell whether a particular word going to piss a Christian off. Hell is both a septic tank for sinners and a naughty swear word—the only thing differentiating one use from the other is context.

But it's also true that if our hero was defeating the actual Satan, that could ruffle some feathers too. The ultimate defeat of Satan is Jesus's job. Is Wisdom Tree trying to create a hero more powerful than Christ himself? Calling Satan the Final Boss offers theological wiggle room—*he's not Satan*, Wisdom Tree could say, *just one of his helpers.*

After Jesus comes back from the dead, he gets the eleven remaining disciples to meet him on a mountain, and there tells them to "go and make disciples of all nations, baptizing them in the name of the Father and of the Son and of the Holy Spirit, and teaching them to obey everything I have commanded you" (Matthew 28:19-20).

This brief speech, known as the Great Commission, is so important to Christendom that it was grafted onto the Book of Mark long after Mark was written so that Mark, a prickly gospel that ends in fear and confusion, would have a happier ending more in line with Luke and Matthew. In the speech, Jesus sets Christianity apart from Judaism by telling Christians it's their responsibility to convert nonbelievers. God's chosen people used to be a tribe, a bloodline; now it's whoever signs up.

Since then, Jesus's message of inclusion has been twisted by governments to justify violent power grabs like the Crusades, the Spanish Inquisition, the slaughter of the Native Americans, and the American invasion of Iraq. But Jesus had no interests in telling governments what to do—he asked his followers to play nice, "give to Caesar what is Caesar's," and then hope Caesar goes away so you can do your thing in peace.

But the Great Commission has also been twisted by Christian tradition into a scare tactic: If you don't follow Jesus, you spend an eternity writhing in Hell with no hope of vanquishing Final Boss. Never mind that Jesus himself never bothers to stress this terrifying reality, or that only a tenth of our notion of Hell itself actually comes from the Bible. Eight tenths comes from Dante's *Inferno*, while the final tenth is split between *Bill and Ted's Bogus Journey* and the "Spooky Mormon Hell Dream" scene in the musical *The Book of Mormon*.

The Hell myth circulates so widely because fear works. It's Christianity's creepy trump card. If those lava pits are *that* hot, I'd better be a good boy. If those pitchforks are *that* sharp, I'd better show everyone how to avoid it.

The closest I ever came to saving someone from the fires of Hell was the time in high school I became fast friends with a girl named Megan. We kinda liked each other, and she opened up to me about the problems she had with her mom and an older ex-boyfriend. But since I only dated Christian girls, I parlayed our mutual attraction into inviting her to youth group with me. She became my project.

For a little while the project went surprisingly well. Megan rode with me to youth group meetings, met my friends, and asked lots of heavy questions. But after a while it became clear to her that she and I weren't going to happen, and when her attention diverted elsewhere, she found better things to do on Wednesday nights. I felt like shit. In my head I'd been her one big chance at salvation, and I'd blown it: A better, bolder Christian would have known how to win her soul. When I saw Megan around school after that, I felt so much guilt that I had a hard time even saying hi.

I now believe that the reason to feel bad about Megan and all the beachgoers at SEMP was not that I hadn't won them over for Christ, but that I'd seen them as potential converts instead of as people. Megan rightly ended her friendship with me for the same reason you might need to end a friendship with a woman who has begun selling Mary Kay—her group of friends has overnight been transformed into a network of potential customers. Her eyes are full of pink caddies.

•

Spiritual Warfare is the lone game that resists Ian Bogost's otherwise fair critique that Wisdom Tree games "did not proceduralize religious faith." Whereas *Bible Adventures* merely gamifies Bible stories, *Spiritual Warfare* suggests a more intimate understanding of Christian culture, integrating not just biblical tropes but contemporary Christian ethics into gameplay.

In the city, you encounter something you'd never see in a licensed NES game—a building marked "BAR." Not a café, not a soda shop, a real bar. Enemies flood out of the bar's open doors as you approach, running past you as if for their lives.

Rule #1 of open-world adventure games: Go through every door. A creature might now and then charge you a few rupees to pay for the door you just bombed, but maybe something essential will happen—an item or clue that points the way forward.

Rule #1 of navigating the real world as a Christian: Don't go through every door. Drinking's bad, bars are lusty, and bar-gals are loose.

My high school Christian Club used to trot out these discussion cards featuring ethical riddles. One I remember was, "Are there circumstances under which you'd consider being a bartender?" and then some kids would say, "Well it could be a ministry opportunity, and I could cut people off before they got *drunk*-drunk, and I wouldn't drink myself..." and others would say, "The correct answer is NO. To work there would be to endorse it, and I think if Jesus showed up and saw you selling alcohol to people in a bar, it'd make him *pretty sad*. Whether you were being 'nice' to the drunks or not."

But *Spiritual Warfare* is a video game. So you go into this BAR to see what the chatty barkeeper might have to tell you, and are faced, instead, with an angel. Fuck. "You have no business in a bar," he tells you. You notice that this bar contains nothing: No chairs, no tables, no patrons, no bar. Just the angel and the text of his admonition. "As punishment," he continues, "I am taking back the Belt of Truth. You can reclaim it somewhere in the slum."

Later in the game, you happen upon a tall building with windows that form the shape of a dollar sign: a casino. The old woman standing outside it warns, "You'd be very wise not to enter this building," and this time you understand it's a trap: *Here, there be angels.* And so you wisely move on, allowing this one part of the map to go unexplored, not out of any particular virtue, but for a good Christian's best reason to avoid vices—fear of punishment.

•

That's where this chapter ended until Dan Lawton got back to me with replies to some questions I'd sent him.

When I met Dan Burke for coffee, he said that he'd never gotten a chance to thank Lawton for helping him become an atheist. So when I later emailed with Lawton, I mentioned his role in Burke's conversion, guessing Lawton would be pleased.

Instead, he replied, "I regret what I said to Dan Burke. […] At times I'd find things that modern Christians believed in to be intolerable, especially since I knew the real version of that religion was a lot more interesting […] I probably went off on a rant to Dan Burke one day. And he liked what he heard." Lawton called his anti-Christianity rant "an autistic meltdown," the kind that can be triggered "when you have too many contradictory facts floating around in your head."

"I missed the human side of it," Lawton continued. "Older people with failing health and worries about life who find comfort in believing. There's nothing wrong with that. I just didn't get it at the time." He sounded like me: *I'd seen them as potential converts instead of as people.*

Lawton said he hoped Dan Burke might someday find his way back to religion. "That's the good thing about how this world works," Lawton said. "We're all brought down by aging, and have to rethink things."

So there goes my pithy dinner party story about the godless boss of a "Christian" company who led his Christian employee to atheism. That's the truth for you—always turning simple punchlines into something more complicated.

Maybe it's natural to feel guilty no matter what direction you convert someone. I'll convert people to believing in climate change all day long—it's a verifiable fact. But to pull someone toward or away from God? The best any of us can do is compare notes.

AGING HARDWARE, BUGGY SOFTWARE

DURING THE WISDOM TREE YEARS, Color Dreams never formally went away. Like when a musical side project suddenly becomes more popular than the "main band," Wisdom Tree now gobbled up nearly all the development team's time and attention while Color Dreams languished.

With the exception of one secret pet project. While Lawton and his team were creating sweet Bible games about collecting animals under the Wisdom Tree label, they began a new Color Dreams game called *Hellraiser*, based on a 1987 horror movie of the same name.

The movie *Hellraiser* is about a woman who secretly keeps her undead brother-in-law in her attic, feeding him the blood of men she brings home so that the undead brother-in-law can fully return to life and they can run away together. The plot also involves a puzzle box that, when solved, unleashes a race of creatures called the Cenobytes from their sexy S&M Hell dimension so they can force humans to suffer/enjoy the

Cenobytes' dark erotic lifestyle. Or it would be erotic if the Cenobytes didn't like it so rough that their partners always died. Lawton loved the movie, which had what he called "kabalistic implications," and he licensed the game rights for $50,000.

A *Hellraiser* game needed to be profane, sexy, and above all, bloody, so for *Hellraiser*'s engine Color Dreams acquired the rights to a violent game that that had already changed PC gaming forever: *Wolfenstein 3D*.

In an internet rumor that's more fun than true, id Software released *Wolfenstein*'s source code to Color Dreams/Wisdom Tree for free as revenge against Nintendo for imposing its heavy content restrictions on the SNES version of *Wolfenstein*, scrubbing the game of blood, shootable dogs, and (as mentioned earlier) Hitler. What better way to get Nintendo back than to leak the code to a competitor?

In truth, Color Dreams paid id Software for the engine, and it was a good deal for id, too, who had already made most of the money they were going to make from sales of *Wolfenstein*, and were nearly ready to unleash their next shooter, *Doom*, on the world.

Hellraiser was the most graphically complex game Color Dreams had ever attempted, and it required a specially engineered "super cart." With the help of a San Diego med student named Ron Risley, the team built a new coprocessor—a tiny computer—that added RAM and tripled the Nintendo's processing speed. This allowed for complex graphics and enemy A.I. that had never before been possible on the NES.

Since the super cart couldn't increase the NES's 8-bit color palette, the team attempted to simulate 16-bit color by quickly alternating between two colors in the 8-bit palette. Unfortunately, the colors didn't swap quickly enough for the effect to work.

There were bigger problems too.

Some at the company wondered if the release of *Hellraiser* would ruin Wisdom Tree's Christian branding. "Eddy [Lin] thought it'd hurt our Christian reputation if *Hellraiser* was released," Deforest told me. "I don't think it would have made a difference, personally, but that's one reason *Hellraiser* took so long to develop."

"The company was being managed by people who had never played a video game and never would," Jon Valesh said, "and were not strongly attached to the Western culture which would produce a movie like *Hellraiser*. To expect them to produce a game that was gory enough, sick enough, and mean enough to fit the movie is to expect too much [...] It started out very blue and very red, and then there was less red. Once the red is gone, what's the point of the blue?"

Most importantly, the super cart turned out to be extremely expensive. Each game's price tag would need to exceed $100, and there was no way people would pay it, especially as technology continued to improve. "By the time the first test version [of *Hellraiser*] was ready, *Doom* had already come out," Vance Kozik said, "and the look and feel of the *Hellraiser* game was soon to be antiquated."

The team gave up on *Hellraiser* and let the clock run out on the $50,000 game rights. But surely there was some way they could still use the *Wolfenstein 3D* engine, right?

•

The solution: A new Wisdom Tree game called *Super 3D Noah's Ark* (1994), this one for the SNES.

Instead of taking the *Wolfenstein* engine and putting it toward a new game, Wisdom Tree gave *Wolfenstein* the TABII treatment. They did as little work as possible to turn it into a Bible game, in turn creating one of the most bizarre titles in video game history.

Instead of a WWII spy, you control Noah.

Instead of a gun, you've got a slingshot.

Instead of bullets, you shoot fruit. (Not the Fruits of the Spirit this time, but regular produce.)

Instead of a Nazi castle, you're on the Ark.

Instead of Nazis, you shoot goats, ostriches, sheep, and oxen.

Instead of swastikas, the walls are covered with paintings of animals.

Instead of Hitler, you face Burt the Bear.[13]

The maps, though? Identical to *Wolfenstein*.

---

13   For those counting, that's the third Wisdom Tree game in which the final boss is a big bear.

The ammo/health placement? Identical.

The enemy AI? Identical.

When you shoot an animal, it falls asleep, presumably having eaten the fruit in between frames, now ready to settle down. The "two of each animal" rule, honored by *Bible Adventures*, has been thrown out. In this game's reality, God was obsessed with goats and apparently had Noah fill the Ark with them.

As in other Wisdom Tree games, *Noah* does not directly contradict the Bible so much as it fills in the margins of a story about which we are told nearly nothing, since there is not a word in the Bible about how Noah and his tenants spend their time on the Ark. Genesis 7:16 says, "Then the Lord shut him in," and 40 days later, in Genesis 8:6, Noah opens a window and sends out a raven. Who's to say he *didn't* go on a fruit-shooting rampage?

Still, *Super 3D Noah's Ark* is different enough from both the Bible and *Wolfenstein* to be wholly incomprehensible, which may be why it didn't sell very well in Christian bookstores upon its release. This was the first and last game Wisdom Tree would make for the SNES, and in fact was the only unlicensed game ever to be released for the system. Shooting animals just didn't make as much sense as collecting them.

But how does it play? Because *Wolfenstein* itself is fun, *Ark* is fairly fun too. The gameplay is simple and the graphics are pixelated, but the well-designed *Wolfenstein* maps are sprawling and full of mystery.

It's the hit detection that frustrates. It's tough to tell how well your slingshot is working against the rabid ostriches, or how one slingshot differs in power and range from another. Likewise, men who used to shoot you have been replaced with animals who merely kick you, yet somehow those animals can kick from great distances.

•

Flawed mechanics create challenges that were never intended by a game's creators. You find yourself asking not, "Why is this opponent so hard?" but instead, "Why didn't the dumb game do the thing I told it to?"

What makes *Bible Adventures* such a challenge for speedrunners like Brian Lee Cook are the game's imprecise physics—the difficulty of controlling your character. "I think we're generous when we call them 'physics,'" Cook notes, "because they hold no resemblance to anything that could function in a world, real or imaginary." He singles out the simple mechanics of running, jumping, and picking things up. "The game feels slippery enough that the ground should have been covered in ice. It's terrible. Because of this, it's difficult to calculate jumps or even pick up the baby who longs for the river. When too many objects appear on screen, the lag is so bad that it's difficult to pick anything up. Often, I end up throwing what I want to keep."

Most of the games made by Color Dreams/Wisdom Tree were created in a programming language Dan

Lawton invented called "state machine," which the team renamed BOGUS, an acronym for nothing at all. State machine allowed developers to create new games without having to reprogram the mechanics from scratch, just as new first-person shooters make use of Unreal Engine today. "It allowed designers to make entire games, down to the level of character behavior, with little or no programming background," Kozik explained. "The side effect was the game response time was often very slow and jerky."

A perfect example is the Color Dreams game *Challenge of the Dragon* (1990), which dares to ask: What if *Double Dragon* looked worse, had awful controls, and featured an impenetrable second stage where lasers shot at you from nowhere while you were asked to navigate a series of punishing timed jumps? A shameful attempt at brand confusion, *Challenge* is truly the *Snakes on a Train* of video games. Which would be completely forgivable if it was fun to play.

Even worse was when the state machine's limitations were combined with game design inexperience, as was the case in Color Dreams's 1991 Indiana Jones homage, *Secret Scout in the Temple of Demise*. Originally called "The Aztec Game," *Scout* followed a Boy Scout trying to escape the Amazon jungle.

Plagued by the same swarm of control problems that afflicted most of the Color Dreams games, *Scout* was challenging in ways both intentional and accidental: When facing an enemy, you fling yourselves at one another until one of you dies. Often, your main task is simply to dodge spears flung at random from offscreen. Arrows come flying from natives in windows. In an early temple, you're seized upon by sets of three messy-haired boys who throw candy at you, and the best way to kill them is to trick them into dumbly jumping off a cliff.

Early in the game's development, Deforest had the idea to create health hearts that randomly exploded—not unlike the devious poisonous mushrooms in the original Japanese version of *Super Mario Bros. 2* that we in the West call "The Lost Levels," but without a way to tell the difference between the actual power-ups and the deadly ones. Deforest was mercifully steered away from this idea, but most of his other deadly traps made it in the game.

When I asked Deforest why *Scout* and other games from the NES era were so unrelenting, he didn't try to speak on behalf the developers of his time—didn't whisper of the lost arts of challenge, pattern recognition, or a truly *earned* victory. "To be honest," he said, "I didn't know how to make a fun game. If the game was challenging to me, I figured it'd be challenging to others. Vance [Kozik] even mentioned that the first level of *Secret Scout* was too hard, and I should ease the player into the difficulty of the game. I don't think I heeded his words, because I really didn't know that would be an issue."

What do the Color Dreams/Wisdom Tree games lack? Ultimately, not graphics, which even at their worst are passable (unless you count the Sega Genesis ports, which are truly behind the times). They don't lack concept, either: Spacemen shoot lasers at creatures, trenchcoat cops shoot bullets at druglords, a Bible character in a rioting ark shoots fruit at animals. Great! Whatever!

To me, the thing that keeps these games from being quite as fun as many of their licensed competitors is what game designer Tim Rogers calls "sticky friction." According to Rogers, what the best games have in common is a "jaw-dropping, fantastic, insane, meticulous, obsessive attention to detail when it comes to the weight, friction, and existence-sense of its characters." I'd previously only heard Rogers's concept referred to in old game magazines as "play control" or the more ambiguous term, "the feel of the game."

In a Kotaku manifesto, Rogers writes,

> That's why people played *Mario*. If you asked a space alien from the future to play *Super Mario Bros.*, and then play any of the other sidescrolling platform games of that era, and then report back to you with one sentence on what he perceived as the major difference between the two, he would speak gibberish into his auto-translator, and it would output a little piece of ticker-tape with the words "STICKY FRICTION" printed on it. It is the inertia of Mario's run that endeared him to us. It didn't have anything to do with brand strength or graphic design. Those things were secondary. It was all about the inertia, the acceleration, the

to-a-halt-screeching when you change direction. You can feel the weight of the character.

Before the sequels, before the cartoon, Mario was a little collection of humanish pixels who felt great to control. I look back on all the games I loved most fiercely from that era—*Mike Tyson's Punch-Out!!*, *Metroid*, *The Legend of Zelda*—and the next—*Sonic the Hedgehog*, *Donkey Kong Country*, and the great unsung *Rocket Knight Adventure*—and what united them is sticky friction. It's what set them apart from otherwise great also-rans like *Kid Icarus*, a game that requires countless timed jumps from its player but fails to provide the tools (such as a hold-B-to-run mechanic) that make such games fair and fun.

When the badass sometimes-Christian skatepunk of *Menace Beach/Sunday Funday* attacks a muscled weightlifter and you have no idea whether one or both or neither of you will take a hit, that's a failure of sticky friction. When a spear-wielder makes no visible contact with Moses's mom, but you take a hit, drop your baby, and he throws it in the river, that's a failure of sticky friction.

When a growing legion of us fail to shut up about the brilliance of *Spelunky*, what's most praiseworthy (even more than the roguelike level generation) is that the little big-nosed explorer is one of the most responsive videogame characters of all time, that his response to his environment (and his environment's response to him) feels *right*, and that when we die (and die, and die), we die never because of the game's failures but because of our own. Without this level of responsiveness, we players would lose the drive to improve. And unlike in games where improvement is mostly about memorizing enemy location, improvement at *Spelunky* is all about cataloguing and refining a series of responses to myriad situations—doing a cost/benefit analysis of every danger and prize and acting accordingly. As Penny Arcade's Ben Kuchera once tweeted in one of my favorite things anyone has ever said about a video game, "*Spelunky* features a robust leveling and XP system, but it exists only in your heart."

●

The greatest games mimic life, but not in the graphically realistic way we always talk about. In fact, I've always had a hard time caring about a game's realistic graphics because "the closest possible approximation of reality" is not a thing I ask of any art form, be it games, movies, or books.

What really matters is that a piece of art *feels* like life—that it be so responsive, so considered that there must be a human behind the decision. It's why genius/monster Steve Jobs reportedly kept the original iPod's engineers up all night until the headphone jack made the right *click* sound. Sticky friction was both achievable and difficult in the 8-bit era, and it's both achievable and difficult now. It's no wonder Wisdom Tree had such trouble getting it right.

And yet. While the best games gain their personality from completeness, from considered-ness, from purity of vision, the Wisdom Tree games feel personal because they're such a glorious mess. Just as I'd rather watch *The Room* than *Horrible Bosses 2*, just like I'd rather read a short story by an eight-year-old than a short story by an eighteen-year-old, I'd rather spend time with *Bible Adventures* than with a coldly proficient shooter like *Tom Clancy's Ghost Recon: Future Soldier*.

The ironies of the Wisdom Tree story are many, and are often deployed online for cheap laughs: A Christian company makes *unlicensed* games! Secret atheists make *Christian* games! These "peaceful" Christian games sure are *violent*! But these dualities in both the games' story and the games themselves make Wisdom Tree's body of work not just funny but human. Wisdom Tree's unique combination of ambition, laziness, faith, faithlessness, tools, constraints, sincere desire to make good games, and opportunism produced a series of works of art that are equal parts accident and intention. At their best these games are the Daniel Johnston of their medium—off their meds in a good way. They're also the product of an era in gaming, Christianity, distribution, and culture that had never existed before and will never exist again.

Taken together, the Wisdom Tree games are more singular, more distinct than the output of nearly any studio of their time. And occasionally they're even kinda fun to play.

#RETROGAMING

BY 1995, THERE WERE NO MORE NEWS articles telling Mario to move over for Noah. In the only piece of relevant journalism I could find from this time, a Christian bookstore owner admitted that the Wisdom Tree titles were "not exactly jumping off the shelves."

Part of the problem was that the Christian bookstores that had flourished for decades were now beginning a steady decline that continues to this day. According to a report from Cathedral Consulting Group, the decline began in the early 90s when Christian singers like Amy Grant crossed over into the mainstream. While this meant that the Christian bookstores now sold something everyone wanted, it also meant that music stores now understood there was profit to be found in creating a Spiritual (or, more euphemistically, Inspirational) section. Other markets dipped as well, as photocopies now simplified the use of sheet music and projectors replaced hymnals in churches. Eventually, there were more Christian books stocked in the Christianity section of a Barnes & Noble than there were in an entire Christian bookstore. And then the internet arrived.

Amazon crushed book retailers. Piracy crushed the music industry. Every translation of the Bible became searchable online. The number of Christian stores in the U.S. went from 4,000 in the mid-80s to 2,800 as of 2008 and with more closings since then.

For Wisdom Tree, meanwhile, the cost of making games rose as technology progressed. With each successive generation, mainstream games required more and more developers to work longer and longer hours. The niche Christian audience who'd bought *Bible Adventures* couldn't make up the losses if Wisdom Tree were to attempt an original Sega Genesis game, let alone a PlayStation game. "We just couldn't afford to make the games anymore," Lawton said.

It was time to call it quits.

In early 1997, Lawton and Lin sold Wisdom Tree to Brenda Huff and her husband. Lawton described the sale as "a handshake type deal" in which Huff could sell the Wisdom Tree titles, "but if we wanted to put the games into something new, we also could do that." Already on to the next idea, Lawton never wanted to. He instead formed StarDot Technologies, which to this day makes digital cameras, and brought some members of the Wisdom Tree development team like Vance Kozik along with him.

Dan Burke, Robert Bonifacio, and Roger Deforest all went on to work at Mindcraft, where they developed *Tegel's Mercenaries* and its sequel, *Strike Squad*. Deforest described Mindcraft as "my favorite time during my small stint in the video game industry," but the company folded shortly after *Strike Squad*'s release. Deforest now lives in Fresno, CA, where he works as a Systems Engineer in healthcare IT. In his free time he's writing a sci-fi novel that's as weird as anyone who's played "Free Fall" would expect. "I don't want to give too much away," he said, "but it involves a space donkey. Who talks Esperanto." Deforest and his son are together developing a sequel to *Secret Scout* for the Android.

Burke is the only member of the Color Dreams development team to have remained in the industry ever since. He worked on a game called *Siege*, which Blizzard later told Dan was one of the inspirations for the original *Warcraft*, and he has more recently been making mobile casual games for iOS.

Brenda Huff continues to sell the remaining Wisdom Tree cartridges from an exceptionally 90s-looking website, wisdomtreegames.com, where all the old Wisdom Tree games are available to purchase for the PC or to play for free in Java. You can also buy newer games like *Jesus in Space*, where you play astronauts who, upon discovering a new race of aliens, must figure out how to convert the aliens to Christianity.

•

Christian game development has shrunk and grown since Lawton's team called it quits. While no Christian games have approached the success of *Bible Adventures*, there are now many more developers who want to make Christian games.

The Christian Game Developers Conference (CGD) is a gathering of developers who since 2002 have met annually to discuss how game developers might better put their talents to the service of God, hosting talks like "Expressing the Christian Message Through Art," "Narratives in Games and God's Big Story," and "Why Should Christians Care About Games?"

To their credit, the CGD organizers seem painfully aware of the tension between profit and ministry. Half of the "Core Values" on the conference's webpage address the conflict directly. (Emphasis theirs.) "Never, ever, **EVER** market God like He is a product." But then: "A well-run business that makes a profit is a **legitimate** and **appropriate** way to serve God." And on the other hand: "That said—**greed is incompatible** with our understanding of morality."

Wisdom Tree is a member of the conference, and sells games by conference members through Wisdom Tree's online store—games targeted to the very young with titles like *Good Sam* and *Bibleman*.

However, as Patrick Stafford makes clear in his 2012 Polygon article "Higher Calling," CGD is a bigger tent than you'd initially think: While there are guys like Brent Dusing, who wants to carry the Wisdom Tree torch with overtly biblical games like *The Story of Moses*, there are others like Josh Larson, who made a kaleidoscopic Wiimote screensaver game (*Weiv*) to add a new visual element to church services. Lance Priebe (*Club Penguin*) just wants to be a Christian guy who makes good games, no need to include religion at all. Ryan Green (*That Dragon, Cancer*) wants to authentically represent the loss of his child, and for Green that authenticity includes faith. This newer wave of developers seem much more in line with Drew Dixon, editor of Gamechurch.com, when he says, "I think Christian game makers should try to ask interesting questions of players rather than constantly seeking to answer questions."

When I asked Brenda Huff why Christian gaming never took off the way Christian music did, she said, "First of all, it is a hostile market. Getting a Bible-based title licensed is almost impossible. Secondly, cost-to-sales ratio is too high. As the technology has increased, the costs of development and production have gone through the roof. Between a high cost of product and a soft sales base, it is just really risky."

Christian game development has become a fringey and unprofitable art form, like poetry, improv, modern dance, and opera. But if you ask artists within any of these communities why they still bother, they will tell you there is something perversely rewarding about having your chosen art form left alone by capitalism. In 2014, opportunists like Dan Lawton have long since wandered off to make webcams. So when you look around a conference room like the one at CGD, you know instantly that the smiling dudes taking notes in the seats around you *must* be in this for the love of the game or else they wouldn't be here. These are your people. These are the true believers.

•

Wisdom Tree has existed more as a game distributor than a developer since Brenda Huff purchased the company. So it was a surprise when, in January 2014, a company called Piko Interactive rereleased playable SNES carts of *Super 3D Noah's Ark*.

Piko came to Huff and asked her if they could manufacture the carts, and now the game is selling for $65 through both Piko and Wisdom Tree. "There have been numerous inquiries over the years," Huff told me. "With Piko, everything clicked."

Stephen Georg of the YouTube channel StephenPlays filmed an unboxing of the game. And with the exception of several syntactical errors on the back of the box, the game cart and its packaging, shrink-wrap and all, look very professional—like a real game.

And in the case of *Super 3D Noah's Ark*, the new version looks better than it ever has before. The original cart was designed as a pass-through: As if using a Game Genie, you had to attach *Noah* to an existing SNES cartridge for the game to work. The licensed game would disable the Super Nintendo's security chip, then the machine would play *Noah* instead of the licensed game.

So how is a game that barely sold on its initial release honored with not just a rerelease but an upgrade?

When I asked Brenda Huff how she'd seen the legacy of Wisdom Tree change over the years, she first talked about the good years with NES, the successful rereleases onto PC, Game Boy, Sega Genesis, and SNES, and then a long lull. "When my husband and I purchased Wisdom Tree, it was on the downward spiral. For a few years we could not give NES games away. […] Being an eternal optimist with a touch of hoarder, I kept the parts and pieces of the games, and all the other things that made Wisdom Tree work. Then retro gaming came along."

Retro gaming—aka classic gaming or old school gaming—is the playing and collecting of old video games. But it's not just that: It's a t-shirt of an NES controller. It's a specifically *SMB1* Mario tattoo. It's the hashtag epilogue to a tweeted photo of the weekend's garage sale vintage game haul. It's an indie game developer who opts for her game to employ heavy pixelation when she has the tools to make it smoother. It's a well-attended live *Battletoads* speedrun. It's dancing to chiptunes at Indiecade. It's the 45 minutes of *GoldenEye 007* I played at Jared's after dinner last weekend. It's part of the drive to read/write/publish Great Books about Classic Video Games. Retro gaming is—say it with me now—a lifestyle.

In 2011, Kotaku's Mike Fahey asked, "How old does a game have to be to be considered 'retro'?" Reader responses ranged from "32-bit and under" to "20 or more years old" to any console that has a "distinct feel" and "distinct smell" to "when it has a certain amount of charm" to "the console should be more than two generations old" to "when some hipster has [the game] hanging around their neck." Most readers' answers could be boiled down to Supreme Court Justice Potter Stewart's quote about what constitutes hard-core pornography: *I know it when I see it.*

Retro has always been a moving target. The other day, I was shocked to hear the local oldies radio station playing Cyndi Lauper's "Time After Time," a song that came out within a month of my birth. If "Time After Time" is an oldie now, K-Earth 101 will be playing "Smells Like Teen Spirit" within a decade.

The retrogaming subreddit proclaims, "This subreddit is for those of us who still love the golden-age of video games, before it was all about the graphics." And while it *is* affirming to check in with, say, *The Legend of Zelda*, and confirm its greatness despite/because of the game's pixelation, there are a couple of problems with Reddit's "before it was about the graphics" mantra. (1) It absolutely was about the graphics. The NES distinguished itself by having much higher graphical capabilities than Atari and its contemporaries, and flouted this superiority every chance it got. Then Genesis and SNES did the same thing. Then PlayStation and N64 did the same thing. And so on. (2) Someday soon, retrogaming will have to accommodate games that have terrific graphics. When *Grand Theft Auto V* and *Mass*

Effect 3 are retro, what makes them retro will not be their outdated resolution but simply their age.

Since starting Boss Fight with a mission to let authors pitch games to me instead of my choosing the games for them, I've been fascinated by how many more pitches I've gotten for SNES games than for any other platform or era. In our first exception to our "authors choose the games" rule, we invited readers to vote on the game they most wanted to read a book about. The top four were *Final Fantasy III/VI*, *The Legend of Zelda: A Link to the Past*, *Super Metroid*, and *Chrono Trigger*.[14]

We humans tend to attach ourselves most firmly to the cultural objects we encounter in our teens. When it's time to write a book about a game, there are some rare writers who might immediately want to dive into something they played recently, but most head straight for the cultural sweet spot of their youth.

Many gamers take this nostalgia to the next logical step and track down the retro games they *didn't* play when they were kids, and become collectors. For this reason, an inverted market for old games has arisen in which the games that performed the worst 20 years ago—*Bonk's Adventure*, *The Flintstones: Surprise at Dinosaur Peak*, *Hot Slots*—are now the most collectible. This is how retro games became the baseball cards of our time.

---

14   If you want to get technical, we combined votes for *Metroid* and *Super Metroid*, and combined votes for the original *Zelda* and *ALttP*. But in both cases, the SNES version was the favorite.

So if collecting is the reason everybody wants an authentically old cart of *Super 3D Noah's Ark*, why would anyone order a new one? Are they buying it ironically?

It seems plausible. The first time a lot of people heard of *Super 3D Noah's Ark*, after all, was from Episode Seventeen of the Angry Video Game Nerd's longstanding YouTube series about the worst video games of all time.

The episode, "Bible Games," makes fun of *Super 3D Noah's Ark* alongside *Bible Adventures* and *Joshua*. Even today, eight years after the AVGN video was released, this video and its sequels remain the most widespread cultural reference point retro gamers associate with Wisdom Tree. Whenever somebody posts online about a Wisdom Tree game, it's not long before a commenter goes, "Oh yeah—from AVGN!" Sometimes the commenter will embed the video right there as proof that these games are awful.

But I doubt that ironic hategaming is the full story.

I'd bet that while irony's in there, it's more the self-protective irony that allows an adult to buy something he wants but probably shouldn't buy. "Hey, check out the awesomely bad game I just bought," you tell your roommate when secretly there is nothing ironic about how happy you are to own a shiny new SNES game—as nice and as hopeful of a feeling as it was when you were ten.

In Georg's *Noah's Ark* unboxing, he repeats how long it has been since he's opened a new SNES game. For Georg, the unboxing is the holiest moment in the video—actually playing the game is an afterthought.

In an interview with Eurogamer, Brenda Huff tries answering the question of why anyone might want a new copy of *Super 3D Noah's Ark*: "I think it is a game that appeals to niche markets. To a lot of collectors, it is a piece of video game history. For the Christian community, it is an alternative to the violence and sexual content present in so many games. I have customers who want to play the games from their childhood with their children."

Meanwhile, Piko founder Eleazar Galindo pitches the game as an underappreciated gem. "If you are involved in the retro scene, you'd know that *Shaq Fu* and *E.T.* are considered as the worst video games in all history. I still don't see anything wrong with them. I had fun playing *Shaq Fu* with my cousins. Controls were difficult (one of the reasons it's considered to be the worst game), but we practiced until we were good at it." Galindo sums up, "[*Super 3D Noah's Ark*] was a successful attempt to bring first-person-action-shooters games for smaller kids. I guess that's what the majority of the people do not understand."

But these answers aren't satisfying either. There are plenty of games the whole family can play (nearly everything on the Wii) and there are plenty of first-person games where you don't shoot anybody (*Minecraft*).

Ultimately, the culprit is simple nostalgia. It's why your dad kept his baseball cards until his mom threw them out when he went to college, and it's why you kept your Sega Genesis until your mom threw it out when you went to college.

According to psychologist Jamie Madigan of the site Psychology of Games, the most powerful video game nostalgia is social. "You may reminisce about playing the original *Starcraft*, but chances are you're most nostalgic thinking about throwing down with friends in multiplayer or at least bonding with them over the shared experience of how you each managed the single player campaign."

I think of the time my friend Brian and I worked so hard to get 100 percent on *Donkey Kong Country 2*, the other time we rented a dumb fighting game called *Tobal No. 1* because it came with a *Final Fantasy VII* demo, the time I watched my babysitter K.O. Mike Tyson without ever taking a hit, the time I advised a girl to do something for a lot of points in *Super Mario Bros.* and she said, "I don't play for points, I play to win," the agonizing wait to be helped by the glacial employees at FuncoLand, the hours upon hours of *Mario Kart 64* battles at Cesar's house, playing *Commander Keen* with Clayton in his dad's office, my first time seeing *Sonic the Hedgehog* on a big-screen TV at the Mays' Christmas party, playing *Bust-a-Move 2* with Melanie the summer after freshman year of college, playing *Dr. Mario* with Liz during our first harsh Massachusetts winter, and, yes, of over-the-shoulder *Starcraft* campaigns at Chris's house shortly before he and Sam got so good at multiplayer online battles that I was left behind. Last, I think of what Roger Deforest told me: *It's funny that I mostly remember the people at Color Dreams more than I do the games.*

Let me ask you: If it turned out tomorrow that video games did nothing for your hand-eye coordination, that a night of gaming killed more brain cells than a night of heavy drinking, that sustained gaming made human interactions scarier, and that (why not?) video games made people more violent, would you up and stop playing altogether? I don't think I would. Games are fun. Games are social. Games got into my DNA at too young an age for me to ever quit them entirely.

In this way, Christianity is the retro gaming of my spiritual journey—my thinking has progressed a lot since it came out, but sometimes it's nice to stare into the simplicity of its boxy pixels and pine for a simpler time. If a churchful of people are singing a hymn I know, I'm going to sing along. Whether I believe the words I'm singing is almost beside the point.

•

Late into my coffee date with Dan Burke, a beautiful college student came over from where she'd been sitting a couple of tables away, said she overheard our conversation, and wondered if we'd answer some questions for her Worldviews class. Here, again, I could have asserted myself as a journalist—we didn't have time to help her with her homework; I was chronicling game history here. But instead we both shrugged and said, "Sure."

Question #1: "Do you have a personal philosophy of life?"

Question #2: "What books do you consider to be the most influential of all time?"

Question #3: "What artists in any medium do you consider to be the most influential of all time? And how have they affected you personally?"

Question #4: "If you could pass along a single philosophical statement to the next generation, what would it be?"

Jesus Christ. I sometimes think I'd like a break from the Big Questions for awhile.

But Burke was more than ready to answer, and since I left the recorder running, I'll include his answer to Question #4 here. "Be a good person," he said. "Pursue your dreams. Leave the world a better place than you found it. Think through everything you do—don't blindly follow tradition or authority. Be a critical thinker. If someone says, 'Do X because X is good,' I can actually review X to see if it's good. Not just: 'My parents did it, their parents did it.' What do I actually think about X? Live by—not the Golden Rule—but there's a negative version that actually predates the Golden Rule: Do not do unto others as you would have them not do unto you. And that's the one I like."

She asked me the questions too, and as I struggled to answer, what struck me most was how deeply uncomfortable the questions made me. I fixed my eyes on the phone that had been recording our whole conversation, and felt as if I had so little to say about who I was and what I stood for. I had plenty of *thoughts*, plenty of *opinions*, but Dan Burke was able to articulate his Big Answers in a way I couldn't. And hey—that's not what I was here for. I was an interviewer! A sort of journalist!

But this is what happens with Big Questions: You can never get away from them. You drive to Santa Clarita to interview a smart dude about the little entertainments he made 23 years ago, and you wind up being grilled by a gorgeous young woman about what it all means.

Each time it was my turn to speak, I had no idea what I was going to say. Here, one of the Christians I grew up with would say, "So I just opened my mouth and let the Spirit speak for me." Instead, I did something far less lofty. I winged it—did the best I could with the time I had.

These same conditions—limited time, energy, and resources—have yielded both undeniable masterpieces and the most atrocious works of art you've ever seen, read, heard, or played. But most works, like the games in Wisdom Tree's catalogue, fall somewhere in between. The miracle is that they got made at all.

NOTES

When I quote the Bible in the epigraph and elsewhere, it's from the New International Version. The Wisdom Tree games tended to use NIV too, except for in the *King James* Game Boy "game."

You can read all of Dave Allwein's original interviews with the Color Dreams staff at The Warp Zone (neswarpzone. com/interviews.html) and Martin Nielson's interviews with many of the same developers at NES World (nesworld. com). Nielson tells me his interviews were conducted in or around 1998, and Allwein says his interviews were conducted between 2000-2004.

Quality Control

You can watch footage of the rare Atari game *Red Sea Crossing* on the YouTube channel, Fang Films ("Red Sea Crossing Atari 2600 Gameplay"). For the Nintendo and Atari history, I rounded up the usual indispensable histories of gaming: Stephen L. Kent's *The Ultimate History of Video Games*, David Sheff's *Game Over*, and Jeff Ryan's *Super Mario*. Many of my examples of weird Nintendo censorship and some of my understanding of how third party licensing worked comes from J.J. McCullough's essay, "Nintendo's Era of Censorship."

An Odd Kind of Technology

Additional info comes from "Making Unlikely History at Color Dreams," an autobiographical essay by Roger Deforest that's available at Deforest's personal website, colordreams. rogerdeforest.com. "Christian Retail Industry Research" by Philip J. Clements and Sharon Nolt of Cathedral Consulting Group details the rise and fall of the Christian bookstore. The Association for Christian Retail is at cbaonline.org. Cindy Crosby's quote comes from her article in *Christianity Today*, "How to Save the Christian Bookstore."

Bible Adventures

The original Wisdom Tree demo video is on YouTube, posted by "vgpresskits" under the title, "Bible Adventures NES informational video." Steve Knopper's 2014 *New York Times* article on Sia is titled "Sia Furler, the Socially Phobic Pop Star." Brian Lee Cook's speedruns are archived on YouTube. He runs "Baby Moses" at SGDQ 2013 in the video, "Bible Adventures NES - SPEED RUN (02:27) *Live at #SGDQ 2013*," then he runs "David and Goliath" at SGDQ 2014 in the video, "SGDQ 2014 Bible Adventures Speed Run in 0:02:47 David & Goliath scenario by Brossentia #SGDQ2014." Vintage articles that show how Wisdom Tree was portrayed in the media: Adelle M. Banks, "Video Games Zoom In On Biblical Adventures," *Orlando Sentinel* (3/19/91). Lisa Daniels, "Nintendo Ministry," *Newport News* (12/14/91). *Lodi News-Sentinel*, "David battles Goliath – in video game" (12/14/91). Some Brenda Huff interview material comes from Nick Gibson's 2006 interview with Huff for the site Sega-16 ("Interview: Brenda Huff"), and from Samuel Floyd's 2014 interview with Huff for the site, The Vintage Gamers ("Interview with Wisdom Tree Owner Brenda Huff"). Dan Burke's popular YouTube channel mostly devoted to motovlogging, but he occasionally discusses his career in gaming ("Fresno Road Trip and Interview with Roger Deforest, Former Game-Developer!"). Both Seanbaby "Worst Games" lists are archived at seanbaby.com. Norman Caruso's video about *Little Samson* is on his "The Gaming Historian" YouTube channel, titled, "Little Samson (NES) - The Gaming Historian."

Mining for Treasure

The "Prone to wander…" line comes from the hymn "Come Thou Fount of Every Blessing" by Robert Robinson.

Dreams of a Playable Jesus

Robert M. Geraci's article "Video Games and the Transhuman Inclination" appears in the November 2012 issue of *Zygon: Journal of Religion and Science*. The Chinese *WoW* research came to my attention via Jamin Warren's *PBS Game/Show* episode, "Can Videogames be a Spiritual Experience?" Louis C.K.'s "Rape is not up there…" line comes from Season One, Episode Eleven of *Louie*: "God." The 2007 Clint Hocking blog post that coined the term is called "Ludonarrative Dissonance in Bioshock," and it's on his blog, Click Nothing.

Throw a Bible In It

Relevant to this book are the following *Angry Video Game Nerd* episodes, all of which are Christmas specials: 17, 62, 106. They are titled "Bible Games," "Bible Games 2," and

"Bible Games 3." Watch all three in order and watch a boy grow into a man. The William Hardy Jr. quote is from lads2leaders.com's "Endorsements" page.

Spiritual Warriors

The *Billy Graham's Bible Blaster* joke comes from Season Eleven, Episode Fourteen of *The Simpsons*: "Alone Again, Natura-Diddily." SEMP appears to have been rebranded as Lead the Cause (leadthecause.org) and no longer meets in Southern California. The manual I quote is the 2000 edition of the *SEMP Training Manual* (which I've saved all these years for the right time to write about SEMP), though I suspect the "state of Texas" scenario originated elsewhere. The "Step aside…" *Religion News Service* article is called "Bible Speaks In Bits, Bytes, Bleeps" and is unattributed to an individual writer.

Aging Hardware, Buggy Software

The Tim Rogers Kotaku 2010 manifesto is called "In Praise of Sticky Friction."

#RETROGAMING

The guy who said the games were "not exactly jumping off the shelves" was Jim Pearson, manager of the bookstore Blessings, as quoted in Chris Champion's article "Games Christians Play" in the magazine *Alberta Report*. Piko Interactive: pikointeractive.com. Mike Fahey's Kotaku article is called "When Does a Game Console Go Retro?" The Eleazar Galindo quote comes from the Eurogamer article "How Super 3D Noah's Ark came to be reprinted on SNES in 2014" by Jeffrey Matulef. Stephen Georg's YouTube video is called "Super Noah's Ark 3D Unboxing (Day 1554 - 2/25/14)." Patrick Stafford's 2012 Polygon article about CGD is called "Higher Calling: The New Gospel of Christian Faith." The Christian Game Developers Conference is at cgdc.org. "The Psychology of Video Game Nostalgia" by Jamie Madigan appears on his site, The Psychology of Games.

ACKNOWLEDGEMENTS

I could not have written this book without the generous cooperation of Color Dreams/Wisdom Tree employees Roger Deforest, Dan Burke, Dan Lawton, and Brenda Huff.

Thanks to Brian Lee Cook for explaining *Bible Adventures* to me, and to Jon Irwin whose own book gave me the idea to talk to a speedrunner. Thanks to James Davis, Sara Woods, and Brent Lowry for letting me pick their brains, and to Jensen Beach for cheering me on. Thanks to Dave Allwein of The Warp Zone and Martin Nielson at NES World for interviewing the Color Dreams team before it was cool. Thanks to everyone quoted and cited in this book.

Thanks to Ken Baumann for his smart notes and his perfect book cover. Thanks to Aaron Burch for his many close edits and rearrangements. Thanks to Michael P. Williams for all the research help, and for his generous feedback on multiple drafts. Thanks to Ryan Plummer for his copyedits and clarifications, and to Joseph M.

Owens for his careful read. Thanks to Adam Robinson and Christopher Moyer for making these books look so good on the inside. Thanks to all of the Boss Fight Books authors for lending all your heart, smarts, and street cred to this series.

Thanks to my dad for his faith and to my mom for her doubt—this book is for you both.

SPECIAL THANKS

For making this series possible, Boss Fight Books would like to thank Ken Durham, Jakub Koziol, Cathy Durham, Maxwell Neely-Cohen, Adrian Purser, Kevin John Harty, Gustav Wedholm, Theodore Fox, Anders Ekermo, Jim Fasoline, Mohammed Taher, Joe Murray, Ethan Storeng, Bill Barksdale, Max Symmes, Philip J. Reed, Robert Bowling, Jason Morales, Keith Charles, and Asher Henderson.

ALSO FROM
BOSS FIGHT BOOKS